# THE
# SKELETON
# COAST

# THE
# SKELETON
# COAST

*A Journey through the Namib Desert*

Benedict Allen

PHOTOGRAPHS BY ADRIAN ARBIB
AND BENEDICT ALLEN

BBC BOOKS

*To Katie,*
*who with Paul kept the home fires burning*

This book is published to accompany the
BBC television series *The Skeleton Coast*,
broadcast in 1997.
Produced by Bob Long
and Salim Salam


First published 1997

ISBN 0 563 37181 1

All photographs by Adrian Arbib except those on pages 10, 18/19, 26, 30/31, 34/35, 38, 42/43, 50/51, 55, 58, 59, 71(upper right), 90, 91, 94/95, 110(left), 136, 137, 152, 156, 181, 184, 187, 194, 198 and 207(right) by Benedict Allen; pages 23 and 145(above) Bruce Coleman (Jen and Des Bartlett); page 153(Hermann Brehm); pages 145(below) and 169(Dieter and Mary Plage); and page 115 NHPA (Alberto Nardi)


Photograph on page 2: the expedition at sunset in Damaraland (Adrian Arbib)
Photograph on page 3: Himba boy with goat friend (Benedict Allen)

Map by Line and Line, © BBC Books
Designed by Graham Dudley Associates


Set in 12 point Garamond
Printed and bound in Great Britain by Butler and Tanner Ltd, Frome and London
Jacket printed by Lawrence Allen Ltd, Weston-super-Mare
Colour reproduction by Radstock Reproductions Ltd, Midsomer Norton

# CONTENTS

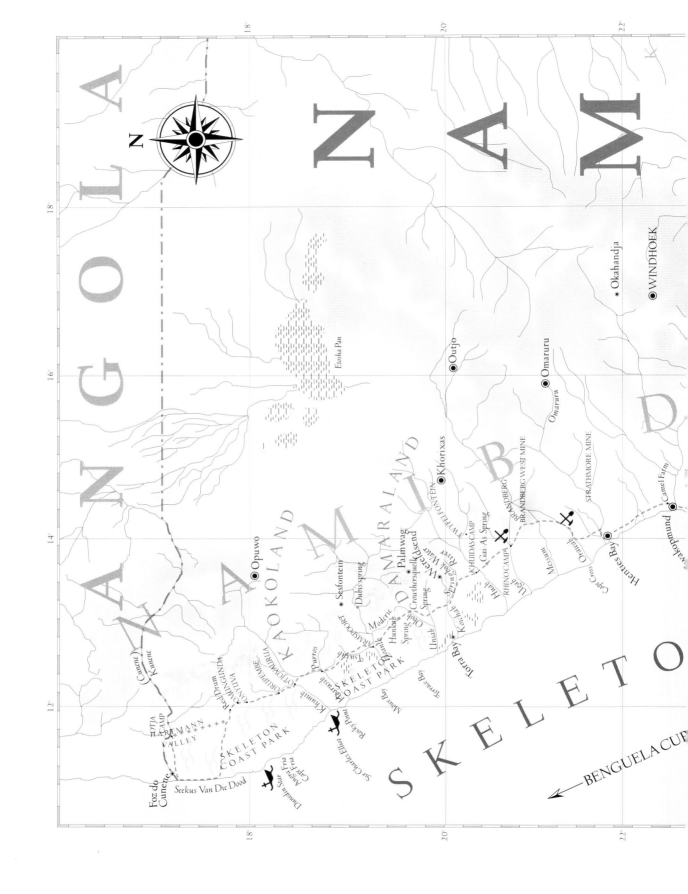

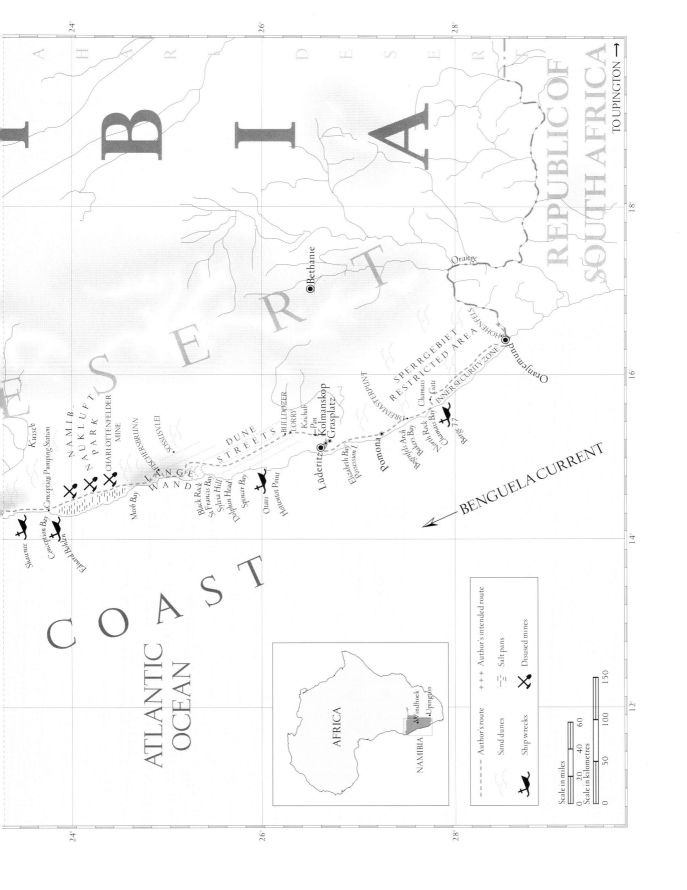

# AUTHOR'S NOTE

My account of this journey is based on extracts from my six notebooks and from three hundred hours of videotape diaries recorded by me for a BBC TV series of six half-hour episodes. This is the first time any remote journey has been documented so thoroughly on television in Britain (and probably elsewhere) so a few thoughts might be of interest.

The advent of the small video camera has made it possible for one person to film a journey without an additional camera operator and this is what I set out to do. The aim was to achieve a sort of raw honesty that would allow the viewer, as well as the reader, to get as close as possible to experiencing the desert: no hindsight, no film crew, just the desert and my unfiltered impressions of it. The dangers of this diary-based approach are obvious. The material, whether from notebooks or small Hi-8 camcorders, tends towards egotism and also lacks objectivity and polish. Diaries can still be manipulated and are also unlikely to provide an educated discussion of, say, social anthropology or wider issues – I'm thinking of the Epupa dam, a construction project that presently threatens the northern Himba people. But the diary approach does, at least in theory, produce a greater intimacy, honesty and immediacy. Whether on paper or videotape, diaries can help cut through received opinion and give a first-hand account, the truth of the moment. As the title and approach of the unorthodox *Mad White Giant* tried to suggest (indeed saying the following was to me the book's point), I think that those we might traditionally have grouped under that dubious label 'explorers' should not simply be challenging scientific boundaries – extending an empire of what is, after all, only a western, rational, understanding of the world – but exploring themes and ideas generated by the place and its people. This anyway will now in part happen: planet Earth is mapped, perhaps not before time our Great Age of discovery is finished. Our own inner minds and consciousness, not other peoples' lands, are the final frontier. The video camera might conceivably contribute by providing an immediate record of impressions undistorted by travellers' written accounts, or at least by the intrusive presence of an accompanying camera-operator/crew and inevitable clobber/fictionalizations. My Amazon programme, *Raiders of the Lost Lake,* was the first such expedition record to be broadcast and is a case in point. Though the diaries were, by careful editing, shaped into rather a High Adventure, in the end this form could be justified by the BBC only because of the quantity of evidence it is possible to gather with a small camera in terms of both real and perceived dangers. Also of importance is the portrayal of indigenous people who have always been the object of our fantasy, originally as noble but savage people and more recently as helpless, wise, 'natural'. As the Amazon project showed, viewed from the personal perspective of a diary, tribal people were able to come across less as subjects and more as ordinary people – the bullies, the bullied, the generous, the manipulative, the manipulated – like us.

In this book, I have added research notes to the diary but have tried not to dabble with the diary unnecessarily. However, inevitably, many incidents and some days have been lost as I simplified and shortened the original account.

The expedition – the first time any journey along the length of the central Namib Desert had been permitted by any government of the country – was a major undertaking and I have many people, mainly Namibians, to thank for its success. I have done my best to mention them all in the Acknowledgements and express my gratitude for being given the privilege to make the journey. On page 210, I have included a brief background history to this exquisite country.

Ten per cent of my total income for this book will be shared equally between Survival International, who have been campaigning on behalf of the Himba, 'Bushmen' and other threatened ethnic groups around the world, and Save the Rhino Trust basecamp at Khowarib, where the three camels that accompanied me on my journey will be used on patrols and to encourage small-scale tourism. The latter is a sustainable project that will allow local people to benefit directly from wildlife and to see the rhino as a greater asset alive.

Those interested in the destiny of the Namib Desert and its inhabitants might like to write to, or support, Save the Rhino Trust, P.O. Box 22691, Windhoek, Namibia, or the UK registered charity Save the Rhino International, 21 Bentinck Street, London W1M 5RP. Alternatively, Survival International at 11–15 Emerald Street, London WC1N 3QL.

# 1

# DESERT APPROACHES

*5 August 1994, Hampshire [After return from River Javari, Peruvian Amazon]*
Borneo, Amazon, New Guinea: year after year I've taken myself off to the world's jungles, ostensibly searching for lost cities, lakes – even a lost ape-man. The rainforest holds an unending fascination to me. But actually this is purely a matter of curiosity – the jungle a billion-piece jigsaw puzzle. I don't think anything out there sticks in my mind so much as the glimpses I've had, usually in passing, of desert. Places not crowded out by fighting vegetation, but just empty scenes of dust. What's this attraction to emptiness? All I can say is, I've noticed that my 'explorer' colleagues see either nothing in deserts or they fall in love with the ethereal spaces, the lack of enclosures. The freedom to exist without walls.

That freedom (or whatever it is) seems to have a hold on some part of me. So I've decided to invest my energy in one of the deserts that have been on my mind.

*1 November, Hampshire*
Thoughts drifting increasingly to an unlikely-sounding place, the Skeleton Coast of Namibia. Shipwrecks litter the beach, and any sailors who escape the South Atlantic and swim to shore find themselves confronting awesome dunes – because

*During a recce, near Terrace Bay. Numerous excursions, by land and air, went into securing the government's confidence in the project. Their eventual permission was given partly because I wished to travel with camels rather than a habitat-damaging vehicle.*

11

this is the Namib Desert, and they've found themselves on what must be the loneliest beach in the world.

The Namib seems to have a complex personality. Its gravel plains are silently still, but its dunes writhe and howl; it's dry, but once a year water surges through its valleys; it's generally hot, yet a cold sea current flows up the desert's western flank, causing chilling fogs to blow inland. Enterprising beetles and lizards sit gathering this moisture before it's blow-dried away. With these thoughts come powerful childhood memories. Dad was trained as a pilot next door in South Africa, and later brought back two weaver bird nests, a stuffed crocodile, and once even a night adder pickled in a bottle of methylated spirit.

I nurtured them – the night adder that needed its meths topped up, the crocodile which had to have surgery when Toffee [the family corgi] chewed off the feet. And the two nests, woven like neatly darned socks. I carefully put them on display in my bedroom and there they sat, year after year, telling me there was something wonderful and magic waiting out in Africa. I'm now thirty-four but these things are still sitting on my shelves, quietly reminding me.

### 7 November

The Namib … Need to spend a few days in libraries sifting the cold, bare facts. For a start, diamonds are scattered in the sands and large sections of the desert are closed to the outside world. Even if I'm given permission, something never given anyone yet, my route would be well over 1500 kilometres – and the dunes alone look impossible.

### 23 November or thereabouts

Meeting at the Royal Geographical Society with a contact of Adrian Arbib [photographer and friend]. From Adrian's description, Bertus Schoeman was a precise, no-nonsense man. A white Namibian bush pilot who'd known the desert since he was six.

Namibia, once the German colony of South West Africa, was taken over during the First World War by its giant neighbour, South Africa, so I pictured Bertus as one of the country's home-grown Afrikaners, a Boer with little time for the blacks – let alone the English and their romantic follies. Turns out he is indeed strong – but quiet, gentle and self-contained. Short silver hair and steady, intense, gemstone-blue eyes.

'Where shall we begin?' I spread my map. 'You've heard from Adrian that I want to go alone?' There was no response. He was studying me with those two bright eyes of his. Silence. 'Alone that is except for some camels?' He was still watching me like an alert desert mammal.

Bertus said simply, 'We have some of the highest dunes in the world …'. One sentence from him, and my plan already seemed in danger of crumbling. 'You don't want any companions? No vehicles?'

I pressed on, a little hesitantly now, telling him that in the Amazon and New Guinea I'd always gone alone and without technology, and instead tried to learn something from tribal peoples. It did seem to work.

He smiled, but not unkindly. Maybe even recognized a bit of me in himself. He said, 'Then of course you must try to go with just your camels, if that's what you want.'

Bertus began drawing all over my map, listing the major problems I'd face. No geographical features among the dunes to fix a compass bearing on; obscuring fogs; almost no springs in the south; prowling lions in the north. There was one way through the high dunes, and that was to duck down to the Lange Wand [Lang-a Vant].

'What's that?'

'You could translate it as the Long Wall. Where the dunes meet the sea. To continue north, you'll have to run along the beach at their base – trapped by this wall of sand – before the tide comes in.' This sounded quite fun – until Bertus told me the Lange Wand was 70 kilometres long. 'How far can a camel do in a day?' he asked.

'Between 30 and 40 kilometres,' I said, guessing wildly. The figure was based on my rather short stint with camels among the Gabbra [of the Chalbi Desert in Kenya] a few years ago. The Gabbra people were a tough nomadic bunch who'd have stayed well clear of this 'Long Wall' had they heard of it. Their desert is a smooth pan, not a wave-smashed beach nicknamed 'the Skeleton Coast'.

Bertus said that of course, these physical problems aside, the reason why no one had done this journey was because of permission. The problem is both the diamond-rich Sperrgebiet, the 'forbidden zone', and the Namib-Naukluft Park, which is restricted because of other, presently unused, diamond fields but also because it's ecologically delicate. Together these two areas make up half of Namibia's desert. There was also the Skeleton Coast Park in the extreme north – nowadays the region usually referred to as the Skeleton Coast, a label originally applied to the coast more generally and coming from a 1933 article in the *Cape Argus* covering the story of the latest disappearance out there. 'To be allowed in any of these areas, you must prepare your case to the last detail,' Bertus concluded. 'Convince the government that you won't ruin the tourist industry by dying out there.'

*Dusk view over the Koichab, north-east of Lüderitz. No aeroplane vapour trails, no vehicle tracks: the desert's very emptiness is its worth to man. Immersing himself there, he has the rare chance to stand back and take a good look at himself.*

### 24 November

Adrian – who's trekked with George [Monbiot, environmentalist] and whom I want to involve in this project because he's genuine through and through, a photographer without the common predatory hardness – has put me in touch with another of his hot contacts in Namibia. He's called John van Bergen and is best known as an international model – his hair flows in long, blonde spirals, and he's often photographed with beaches and surfboards. I do hope he knows something about camels – because finding three of them is my next job.

Need encouraging news to pass on to my Mum. So much for the 'mystery virus' that the specialists originally diagnosed for her. It's cancer of the colon.

### 27 November

So far John has found only eight camels in the whole of Namibia. They're owned by an eccentric-sounding German woman, Elke Erb. She says the camels are her family, and she can't let them go. I pictured her fondling the camels as they snuggled around her, relaxing indoors on a hearthrug, safe from the desert winds.

News is bad about Mum. Operation failed to remove all the cancer – she'd

wanted me sheltered from the news until I'd had the launch of my Amazon book at the RGS. Radiation treatment beckons. If she doesn't pull through, what of Dad? She is his entire world. Mum is also my foundation stone – all mums are special, but she's been the rock beneath my expeditions, though each journey worries her sick. Feel myself looking around desperately for something else to cling to. Do I believe in myself enough to pull this journey off without her?

I'm trying to get the measure of this desert. It's a narrow tract of land, usually less than 200 kilometres wide, extending 1900 kilometres up the coast from the Olifants River in South Africa, through the length of Namibia and to the district of Namibe in southern Angola. My aim is to walk through the heart of the desert, the length of Namibia – that is between the Orange River (South African border) and Kunene (the Angolan).

### 30 November

On phone to Mum. We talked about my coming journey, pretending everything was normal. She said, lightly, 'I gather camels are not very nice people.'

More on the Namib, this place I must learn to understand. Its exact age isn't known, though it's probably the oldest desert in the world. The region seems to have been arid for more than 80 million years, though desert conditions are maintained today largely by the Benguela Current, which was established only 5 million years ago. A permanent anticyclone over the South Atlantic, which blows year-round southerly winds up the coast, result in surface water currents to which are added upwellings of deep, cold water. The resultant 'Benguela System' moderates the temperature of the desert, with cool, stabilizing air on the one hand providing life forms with a vital source of water in the form of fog, and on the other reducing the turbulence that is vital for convectional rainfall.

John (who, as Adrian promised, is indeed a truly inspired organizer) searching for camels – he's now ringing round farms in South Africa, hoping for a forgotten Kalahari beast or two. Rang Gert Behrens, a Namibian who's had experience with camels. Told him my plan. Would they handle the dunes?

'Forget it.'

Would they be able to get along the Lange Wand before the tide came in?

'Forget it, forget it, forget it.' We'd be crushed against the dunes by the incoming tide. If we didn't drown, the sharks would get us.

Rang Mum. Difficult to know how she stands – she only asks me about myself.

### 3 December

John on the telephone: 'We have camels.'

'You're sure?'

'Yes indeed. I don't know what condition they're in, but we now have camels.'

These turn out to be at a Kalahari outpost. But it's something to tell Mum.

Rang the owner of the camels. Rather a forthright man, who sounds like a traditional Boer (a word which anyway does mean 'farmer'), and his farm's north of Upington in one of the old Afrikaner heartlands. He has three, possibly four, camels for sale. Like those used by the Germans in Namibia's pioneer days, they're dromedaries, the light, one-humped camels bred by Arabs for riding. Most were imported to South Africa a century ago for patrolling the Kalahari frontier, and when the remote police station at Witdraai finally gave up the patrols around 1951 they were taken in by neighbouring farmers.

'Can you tell me a bit about those you have for sale?'

'One is called Nelson,' Mr Knoesen said. He added, rather unenthusiastically, 'He's named after our new President.'

'What's he like?'

'Nelson is big.' He paused, thinking about it. 'Very big.'

There's also Jan and Skerpioen – which I fear means 'scorpion'…

### 8 December

I've closed my files – 'Camel Medicine', 'Camel Food and Water', etc. to be with Dad at home. Visited Mum in the Hampshire Clinic. Braced myself before I went in – my mother reduced from a rare inspirer to a pallid dependant. Her face still positive, despite it all. She's always admired Joyce Grenfell, someone who typically stepped forward when meeting people. And she's much the same. A listener, but no time for the second-rate, for people not genuine. Told her about the camels, about how wonderful the desert sounded. Reminded Mum that I'd dedicated my first book to her, 'my prop, pillar and support'. I said to her, 'Now it's my turn to be yours.'

### 17 December or thereabouts

Brought Mum from the clinic to be at home. Put beside her bed a little quote that I'd scrawled on the back of an envelope from one of her get well cards. 'How far that little candle throws his beams! So shines a good deed in a naughty world.'

### 9 January 1995

Mail pouring in, paying tribute to Mum. At the service, the vicar summed her up with beauty and grace. 'A force for good, decency, integrity … ' I read from *The Pilgrim's Progress*. '… So he passed over, and all the trumpets sounded for him on the other side.'

Now I'm meant to be getting my head together and cranking up my expedition machine. But I'm fed up with 'being brave', 'being positive', as people tell me I'm being. When I arrived back at my desk at the BBC I found a bowl of fruit sitting on it – a present from Bob Long, Patrice, Salim, Amir and the rest of the Unit. Deeply touched. The tears I've held in so long were brimming.

### 31 January

My application for permission is being scrutinized by Bärbel Kirchner, head of Namibia Tourism at the High Commission. She is being wonderful, helping me achieve the right tone for the project. After all, why should I be allowed to do a journey forbidden even to Namibians? Perhaps because I can publicize Namibia and my camels won't leave scarring tyre tracks. But this is a rightfully proud country, only free from South Africa for five years, and now governed by a multi-party democracy led by the ex-Freedom Fighters SWAPO [South West Africa People's Organization].

*Overleaf: Perhaps the most formidable obstacle of the lot, the Lange Wand, or 'Long Wall', where for 70 kilometres the huge dunes of the Namib-Naukluft meet the Atlantic. To avoid the dunes we would have to cut down to the shore and make as much headway as we could – before the tide caught us.*

*17 February*

Permission granted! However, 'certain conditions' attached … I'm to fly to Namibia to attend a meeting with the Permanent Secretary and some senior nature conservation officers. I still need to get permission to go through the forbidden diamond area, the Sperrgebiet, which is controlled by Namdeb [the diamond company jointly owned by De Beers and the Namibian government].

*24 February, Windhoek*

Africa's biggest problem is water, and Namibia's problem is worse than most. This is meant to be the wet season, but flying down the centre of the country I see only flat, sparsely vegetated ochre, like a discarded slab of red sandstone, the bushes resembling shrivelled black lichen. The area of Namibia which falls below the 100-millimetre rainfall line is classed as desert – and that's a quarter of the total land area. It's the only country in the world actually named after a desert.

Bus to Windhoek, the capital. Its surrounds are brown Spartan rock, the occasional trees like tired feather dusters – grey, wrecked. The land powdery, scorched – like left-overs. The city, though, is spick and span, showing its original German pedigree. Doesn't seem to be African at all – none of the hawkers, beggars and lost souls of every other African capital. Where's the shanty? The answer lies in part in Katutura, the township left from the South African apartheid era, when the problems were bottled away; but also in the fact that this is an empty country of about 1.5 million people. Windhoek's population is only 185, 000 – a little town. Even if the rural poor do at last flock in with all their dreams, there simply aren't that many of them. For now, those that do come find no work, and, after a couple of weeks sponging off cousins, retreat back up country. Streets remain safe, life unhurried yet efficient.

Went straight to the Kalahari Sands Hotel for an emergency rendezvous with Bertus – last-minute advice before my meeting with the Permanent Secretary tomorrow. Elvis Presley singing on a loop of muzak, weary flight crews booking in at reception. Around us sit black and white men in suits having business meetings over coffee, all arranged in tribal groups – Germans who tend not to mix with Afrikaners, who tend not to mix with the English; Ovambos who tend not to mix with the Hereros, who tend not to mix with … Yet the most striking thing of all about Namibia is the extraordinary absence of conflict since independence.

Bertus warned me again that my security would be the government's biggest worry. I must try to pre-empt any conditions they might impose. He was positively beaming about the project. 'I want this to happen. I want to be involved.' If all goes well at the meeting he'll fly me about the desert to give me a feel for it.

I went to the hotel loo to change into my suit and tie, Superman-like. Then walked up the hill past the sandstone Christuskirche, Church of Christ, a building that looks like it was designed in fairyland. It was built as a 'peace monument' in 1910, the Hereros having been all but destroyed by the Germans. Kaiser Wilhelm II thoughtfully donated the altar windows.

I walked on through the formal lawns and trim gardens of the Namibian parliament building, known in German times as the Tintenpalast, or Ink Palace, because of the amount of bureaucratic scribbling done there. I was directed to an imposing modern block at the side.

The meeting: I was introduced around the table to the government representatives – white, of either German or Afrikaner origin, but thankfully speaking in English, now the national language. Present with the Permanent Secretary, Hanno Rumpf – chain-smoking, quick-talking, nit-picking, incorruptible – were two Nature Conservation officers in uniform. Danie Grobler, silver-haired fox, superficial friendliness – perhaps genuine, but doesn't do a good job of making it clear. Also Tommy Hall, youngish, strong, outdoor man. Too big for this room. Germanic green eyes. Shoulders of a boxer gone to seed.

The PS was smiling grimly at what I was proposing. 'So, Mr Benedict Allen, ja … ' He puffed away, Danie Grobler at his left elbow. Because I'm using camels – they'll even carry my litter – I have permission. However, I would be accompanied through the Namib-Naukluft Park by Tommy Hall.

If this was a surprise to me, it was a shock to Tommy Hall on my right. He began busily rereading one of my 'Expedition Outlines'.

I told the PS I always went alone and that 'exploration' to me was all about trying to leave our own world behind, even our science. The PS: 'If I may be allowed a little dry joke at this juncture, if you get lost out there, the cost in insurance of finding you may finally sink Lloyds.'

We debated some more but I was losing the argument and I began making mental notes about this Tommy Hall. He's no fool. He would've been making notes about me. My assessment of him: forceful, quite methodical, a hint of the military. Needs to lose 10 kilos. His assessment of me: naive, nice, but not up to it. How he got such a track record, God only knows. Needs to put on 10 kilos.

I decided to put this hefty, bearded German on the defensive. Asked if he could ride a camel.

'No, but I am a horseman.'

*Later:* this turns out to be an understatement. He was in the cavalry, patrolling the northern frontier against SWAPO 'guerrillas', who are now the government. He has had thirty-nine engagements with the enemy, whereas most of my own experience with four-legged animals is limited to walking camels in the Chalbi. Among the Gabbra, camels are for carrying things – only babies, old ladies and tourists actually ride them. But this high-powered meeting seemed a bad moment to reveal to anyone that I had never actually ridden a camel before.

### 25 February

Flight at dawn with Bertus and his brother André, who is also a legendary pilot here from 'the war'. They have a family company, Skeleton Coast Safaris, taking tourists by plane into the desert. Together the two brothers seem to know every fold in the dunes, every shadow in the rocks. Our aim today: to inspect the sandy, southern half of the journey, excluding the far south – the Sperrgebiet diamond area which I still need permission for. We were to concentrate particularly on the Namib-Naukluft Park, through which Tommy will – it's been decided – accompany me.

Before long, as we headed south-west, Windhoek gave way to what André called 'farmland'. Looking out of the window, it seemed an outrageous exaggeration. These were biscuit-dry escarpments, striated rocklands – like the last convulsions of a dying planet. Then the dreaded dunes. 'Very soothing to the eye,' someone said of the huge red curving lines. I saw down there serenity, cleanness, untrammelled peace, death. Sudden flashbacks to Mum, who should be gunning for me back home, and is not …

'What you must do,' said André above the engine noise, 'is to follow one of these dune streets.' I could see them clearly, the parallel sand valleys running approximately north–south up the desert. At their untidy, northern end I'd have to scramble through sands down to the beach – the Lange Wand. It was nearing low tide, but in places the seas skidded in, licking the mountainous sand walls. The waves thumped against each other, showing their muscle, spitting foam. It must be noisy down there – the screaming wind, the echo of waves off the sand walls. We flew up and down the coast, seeing where I might escape the tide if I were trapped. 'It is possible, given time,' André said. 'Because anything is.'

### 28 February

Rang Mrs Erb, the woman with the eight camels. Before I could say much, she broke in. 'But these are my pets. I've explained that they won't be suitable for your journey.'

I said I just wanted her advice. Could camels cope with the dunes, if I couldn't manage the Lange Wand?

'Perhaps camels are more intelligent than humans,' she said, proudly. 'They

*On first seeing the camels, the Himba herdsmen of northern Namibia observed, rather unexpectedly, that they were like ostriches* (Struthio camelus). *As time went by, I realized what an acute observation this might be – the good eyes, the sure feet, the long legs for speed and raised head for maximum visibility. Camels are also often compared to horses but in fact, being even-toed ungulates, are more akin to cows.*

know it makes no sense in the heat to go up and down.'

I take this as 'No.'

Reading through the archives, I find that, following the diamond rush in 1908, horses were used quite commonly to help people up and down the coast. Should I drop the camels in favour of horses? But since those days almost all the fresh-water springs have been blown over by sand. That leaves just a well at Fischers-brunn, south of Meob, and a spring on the beach near Sylvia Hill that's reachable only at low tide. My camels will have to do – and camels were, after all, success-fully used by the German police to patrol the southernmost Namib.

At the Bistro [central Windhoek]: just concluded a meeting with Tommy Hall and a second conservation officer, Achim Lenssen, who's the foremost ranger of the Namib-Naukluft Park. With his help we have bashed out a possible route from the Orange River to the port of Walvis Bay ['Wal-fiss' Bay], the first half of the journey. Tommy enthusiastic, boyish. Regards the journey with excitement now. As we talked, I studied this man again. He is in the dangerous anti-poaching game, which puts him up against powerful interests. Yet, I'm told he has an extraordinary loyalty to the people and wildlife he looks after.

## 7 March

Today I've returned from an extended tour with Bertus of the stony, northern half of the journey – Walvis Bay to the Kunene [Koo-nee-nee]. First there are the rocklands of Damaraland – slabs laid vertically, fields of snugly placed boulders. How will I ever get through? I'm seriously discussing fitting shoes on the camels. Beyond these moonscapes and reaching to the Kunene there is Kaokoland [Kao-uku-land], hill and plain country which is also stony but is inhabited by Himba pastoralists. Their presence at least indicates there's grazing for the camels – lack of food being the major reason why I can't simply walk up the western dunes (which hem Damaraland and Kaokoland along the coast) through the Skeleton Coast Park.

## 8 March

The Ministry of Information and Broadcasting has also given permission for what the official letter calls 'this ambitious project'. With the weight of the government behind me, the timing is perfect for my approach to Namdeb, the diamond people, to get them to allow the first-ever passage by an outsider through the Sperrgebiet on foot.

## 9 March

Interview with Abel Gower, executive director of Namdeb, in a top-security building with windows especially angled for viewing diamonds. First some talk, mainly light-hearted, about whether the camels were to be used by me to snuffle up diamonds. Not long ago, guards found a distressed little homing pigeon sitting at the foot of a security fence. Bundles of diamonds were tied to its feet. The smugglers had got greedy – the bundles were so big, the pigeon couldn't fly up over the razor wire. In the worst years 5 to 10 per cent of total production is smuggled out, most through highly organized syndicates. De Beers know the exact quantity because they buy up the diamonds from the black market afterwards.

Suddenly the meeting was over. They 'liked my spirit'. Namdeb will do security checks on me – 'see if you have a criminal record, that sort of thing' – but subject to that, yes, they agree.

For better or worse, my expedition is on. Time to buy some camels.

***12 March***

Bus to Upington, South Africa. I hired a van and drove north into the Kalahari. Red sands appeared. The roadside trees were hung with weaver bird nests. I stopped to examine them, as my father must once have done before choosing two for me. Then I drove on and there were grass hummocks instead of trees and the sand was licking the road. Finally, the sand was the road. Following my written instructions, I turned left across a huge pan. A smooth spread of 100 square kilometres, with black, angular rocks at the far, far side. The car seemed to float over the hot clay, glide through the heat haze. Then up through the escarpment. I paused on the crest. A black eagle turned, pivoting above the van. The farm lay below: Koppieskraal, an oasis occupied by a house, hundreds of bewildered-looking ostriches and, in a kraal, the four camels. I came down the hill quickly, wanting a sneak look at that camel gang, but Mrs Knoesen came out of the farmhouse, and cut me off. After a long drink of water, I went with her for a look.

The camels were doing their best to dodge four black farm workers. The men were calling, 'Koes!', 'Down!' (literally, 'Duck!') and gesturing as best they could with leather halters. They were concentrating their efforts on the biggest camel, which looked as if he'd never heard the word 'Koes' before. I suspected he had.

After a while the camels were fitted with their halters and I watched as the farm workers paraded them in front of me as if I was a dog-show judge.

Mr Knoesen arrived. Face of solid, wind-polished, granite, with an army bush hat. Those domineering, blue Afrikaner eyes again. 'You are satisfied with them?'

'I need a little bit more time …' I said. But when all was said and done, even if they had been the mangiest, meanest camels in the camel world, I would have had to buy them. Where else were there any?

At dusk I came back for another look at Skerpioen and Jan, the two camels I'd now agreed to take with Nelson. 'Why is Skerpioen called after an insect with a nasty sting?' I asked a farm hand.

Eventually, he whispered, 'Meneer … mister, perhaps he used to kick?'

I bet he did.

Jan seems a thoroughly normal camel. Though when he came over for a closer look at me he seemed deliberately to knock over one of the farm workers. Nelson is the natural leader. He's big, but not clumsy – like those fat men you come across who have dainty feet. He shoved his face into mine, in order to assess me better. Then turned away, dismissing me forever. Or so he thinks …

# 2

# PEOPLE
# OF THE DUST

**13 May**

In Walvis Bay with John van Bergen, having spent three weeks visiting Oranje-mund ['Oran-ya-munt'], Lüderitz, Swakopmund, you name it. This expedition has almost run away from me. Too many aeroplanes, Land Rovers, schedules. Just the sort of things that we in the West are proud of – things that have made us 'advanced', things that separate us from the landscape I'm trying to explore. As usual before starting out on a journey, I need to spend time with people who have yet to be unseparated in this way. In this case the goat and cattle herders of the north-west; they know every curve and crack in their land.

**18 May**

I've come with John and his Land Cruiser to Kaokoland in the northernmost Namib to get to know the Himba, and also to have a closer look at the rocks, stones, and other anti-camel inert things. The Land Cruiser is painted in army camouflage greens, with a seal's skull mounted on the front bumper. John rocks his head to cassette music. His sunglasses flashing in the intense light, he lets these desert margins wash over him. As for me, whole landscapes go by as I keep my eyes on the ground, noting what lies in the way of those soft camel feet. Sharp gravels *everywhere* – all looks hopeless, except along the dry stream beds.

*Kwazarane having a quiet ponder. She wears an* erembe, *a crested skin head-dress which normally signifies the status of a married woman.*

27

At Opuwo we stopped to pick up a translator, Petrus, who originally came from the Herero farmlands that we've driven up through. The Ovahimba, or 'Himba People', have a common origin with the Herero pastoralists, archaeological evidence indicating they've occupied nearby Otjitati for some seven hundred years. The Hereros, who settled in more central Namibia, found themselves having to cope not just with the German colonists – who wiped out half their total population in the final stand, at Waterberg – but also with the missionaries. The Hereros – now only 8 per cent of Namibia's population, below that of the Kavangos and the dominant Ovambos – gave up their goatskin skirts and adopted the missionaries' copious Victorian petticoats, dresses and hats. They're still wearing a version of them all these years later, and consider themselves a class higher than the still wandering Himbas. However, in actual fact one of the greatest differences is that nowadays many Hereros work not with their own cattle but with those belonging to white farmers; sometimes it's the Himba who appear to have more reason to be proud.

*Later:* at the Himba settlement of Onyuva, we camp under a mopane tree beside John's Land Cruiser. Half a dozen circular huts stand around a cattle kraal. The young Himba men are away, attending funerals as usual – someone's grandfather always seems to be dying. I've been sitting so far only with the women.

### 19 May

I have three days in which to get a foothold here. Then we leave, and I come back in a few months, just prior to the expedition, to learn from these people how to cope with the emptiness, dust and sun. I'm not perceived as a threat – just a novelty. I'm entertainment in a land of few people – indeed, few-ish life forms. They finger my hair, my shirt, all these alien things, sighing at the speed I scribble in my notebooks, tapping at my pockets to find out what's in them. I spend a lot of time with one young woman, a goatherd, called Kwazarane [Kwa-tha-ra-nee]. There are only nine adults here – one wizen old gent, Wapenga (a middle-aged man who's always preoccupied with his cattle) and seven women. All the women except Kwazarane are considered old – that is, they are nearing fifty.

Kwazarane is about seventeen – round face, dreamy eyes, pleasing laugh. On her head she proudly wears a multitude of plaits created with the hair of any handy relatives or goats. She tends to be a bit mean to her younger female cousin Komogunjera [Komo-gu-njera], who is in the age set two below – a status marked by the wearing of two thick trailing plaits of hair over her face. Kwazarane, who has little decorative scars up and down her chest, is in her prime – and knows it. She easily fends off the predatory glances of Petrus, who was expelled from school for impregnating three girls (his motto is, he says, 'Touch and go').

If I'm known for anything as an 'explorer', it's for sinking into isolated tribal societies. Yet I've got a nasty feeling Kwazarane will always be able to run circles around me. Today she did consent to me walking with her in the rocky hills, rounding up miscreant goats. But of course for the moment she isn't the slightest interested in my (hamfisted) attempts at conversation and just wants to scramble after her goats. 'Ag-ee! Agg, agg!' – sounds like these have blown through these scrublands for centuries. An impatient woman, for someone in a land which seems to have all the time in the world.

Her aunt, Ka-ada [Kar-da], does have time for me, but from her I learn only Himba vocabulary. I need to be up in the hills, to get a feel for the land. But Ka-ada's husband Wapenga is usually busy with the cows – without a herd, life for a Himba man is nothing. Its size carries prestige, honour. Cattle are only slaughtered at key religious ceremonies such as marriage and death, and their home, the kraal, is the sacred and social heart of the village.

And that leaves me with only Kwazarane; I work on her, watch her, trying to be her friend. She throws stones with uncanny accuracy at straying goats – and spins in circles among the flock's dust clouds, singing the only song she seems to know. Out in the hills, she stopped under a tree and – not for my entertainment, I'm sure – began piping on a flute she'd fashioned from a sheath of bark. I got out a tin of pork luncheon meat. As I undid the tin with its key, she ogled at the meat like a child at chocolate: normally, she'd eat nothing more until dusk – she had about a pint of yoghurt this morning – and when it comes to eating meat she stops at nothing. Last night she ate through a whole goat's head including the knotty cartilage of the throat. She used a rock to smash open the jawbone.

*Dusk:* Kwazarane is sitting beside me at her hut entrance, stirring with her finger a mix of iron oxide and clarified butter perfumed with the gum of the omboo, which is both a tree and shrub. In a minute she'll be spreading it all over her body. Dug from the one workable mine in the Himba heartland the iron oxide is highly prized and generally regarded by outsiders to be preserving and moisturizing the skin. I suspect the warm red *otjize* coat gives the Himbas a sense of partnership with the desert. Wearing ochre, they are the same colour as the dusty hills they depend on.

### 20 May
*Dawn:* the air is quiet, the light yellow on our faces; even the goats passive, stilled by the chill of faint mist. K has just sleepily poked her head out of her hut. She is wrapped in a blanket and is now pottering about in it, beginning her first task –

*Right: Dusk at the Himba settlement of Omungunda, in the eastern desert margins, or 'pro-Namib'. Komogunjera and Wapenga (background), by an enclosure for separating off the kid goats, and Ka-ada (foreground, right) talking with a friend. Huts are made from cow dung, spread over a frame of* mopane (Colophospermum mopane) *poles. Quick to assemble, they are also cooler than the 'more civilized' tin-roofed houses now adopted by other remote or rural communities.*

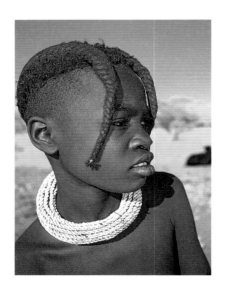

*Above: During my recce period, Komogunjera was the age set two below Kwazarane, and wore her hair over her face in two plaits. On my return with the camels four months later she had been elevated to the status of a senior girl, her face now obscured by a demure curtain of plaits (see page 184).*

milking the cows in the kraal. I'll sit with her, taking her stick and doing what she does – periodically whacking away calves which come to suckle. After that, I'll try to help her shake the milk in a gourd to make yoghurt.

My days are like this: studying this one person who's available to give me a feel for the land, waiting like a hopeless schoolboy for her to be my friend. Unlike the Bushmen, who are nomads, Himbas are, anthropologically speaking, semi-nomads. They simply migrate back and forth between pastures. But they are still elusive, self-reliant, difficult to pin down, and it's hard work for an outsider to get any commitment from anyone.

*Later:* conversation via Petrus, as Kwazarane and I sat making yoghurt, swinging the gourds on a thong tied from a bush. Slop, slop. 'Do you think it's a good or bad custom that marriage partners are usually chosen for girls by their families?'

She wonders about it, playing with the scrap of black plastic bag that she's placed artfully in her hair braids. Surprisingly, Kwazarane talks openly about these matters, as unselfconscious as she is when offering me milk, putting the gourd to my lips. 'It's a good custom,' Petrus said, translating. 'It means that all the other, ugly girls can get husbands too!'

Arranged marriages – especially child betrothals – also serve to teach the young girls the values of society – and obedience.

Deciding Kwazarane's every move is a whole hierarchy of men, ranging upward from the youths who sometimes come visiting the settlement – their heads shaven, except for a central crest which is plaited to form a stiff tail down their necks – to the older men, whose hair is covered in a tight black turban and a skewer affixed for scratching itches within. She is a vassal of her uncle, and he is, in turn, subject to her father, a headman at Okandjombo. Who Kwazarane marries will be decided the day a man approaches her father and the match is agreed by them. She may not hear about it until the day he trots into the village on a mule and takes her away. That's not to say that a marriage would ever be unreasonably forced on a formidable character such as K: if she was made third wife of an objectionable old man she'd only run away and create a family crisis. However, it seems that only senior Himba women have any real clout. At the fireside, Ka-ada will happily chuck a stone at the dozy old man when he's inattentive.

As usual among tribal people, the freedom that we in the West see in these possession-free people is deceptive. They bond together tighter than we can imagine, needing to act as a cohesive force against the desert elements. Nowhere is this seen more clearly than in the role of the sacred fire, surrounded by a circle of stones and guarded by the headman's wife. All domestic fires are lit from this one source, the focal point of village life, and all rites of passage are conducted beside it in order to procure protection from the ancestral spirits living within its flames. When a chief dies, and a heifer is sacrificed on his tomb in the plains, the new chief must make the connection with the sacred flames, bringing the animal's milk back to the village and pouring some on the fire for the ancestors before drinking himself. As I watch this fire I wish I could spend enough time here to understand its strength in the Himbas' lives and the meaning of Mukuru, which is some impersonal power, the 'ancient force', at the head of the long line of guardian ancestors.

### *21 May*

Went to Kwazarane with Petrus to explain that we are leaving for two months. Disappointed to find she doesn't care either way. Nomads: people come, people go. 'You had better not take too long getting back, or I'll be dead,' she says, drily.

John began to pack up camp. I made a huge pot of tea for some passing men who came and squatted, waiting for any hand-outs. They watched us carefully, occasionally relighting their pipes – taking a tinderbox from a pouch in their skirts, then striking a quartz stone for a spark. Tipping back his cowboy hat, John said 'Here's your girl.' There she was, silent and in silhouette against the bleaching midday light, watching from a little way off. She approached silently through the grasses, her beady eyes somehow already on the mirror that I'd carefully secreted in my hand, ready to give her. I slipped it to her and she let out a sigh: 'At-tat-tat-tat …' She said to Petrus, 'Tell him I am very pleased. I will look at myself from sunrise to sunset.'

She will, too. She's fascinated by her face. This is a place with little water. There's only the muddy well in which to look at yourself.

'I have nothing to give you,' she said. Petrus told her to give me one of her bracelets. She had no hesitation, just wondered which to give. It was poignant to see someone part with one of their few possessions so lightly. What else has she got? Just an unmarried woman's garb – iron leg bands, goatskin skirts, the thick neck ring, the conch shell to hang from her neck.

'Your arm is too fat,' Kwazarane complained, squeezing the bracelet on and immediately causing circulation problems.

**Overleaf:** *Kwazarane putting on her morning coat of* otjize, *an ochre dust mixed with butter. Though worn by the women only, it moistens and protects the skin and provides some insulation from extreme heat and cold. Being of a similar colour to the landscape around them, it may also subconsciously bond the Himba with the dusty hills they depend on.*

### 14 July, UK

Final UK preparations – camera equipment, etc. The BBC have somehow calculated that I'll go through five video cameras … I'll be able to power them on the two solar panels they've provided. They expect the panels 'will fit around the camels' humps'.

Sponsorship front mixed. Air Namibia wonderful but everyone else just sees the desert as an exciting new marketplace for their products – me modelling shiny boots, wristwatches. Camel cigarettes are 'talking about sizeable amounts of money'. Declined. Not sure thrombosis, lung cancer and bad circulation are quite my thing.

My final goodbyes at home. Dad looked frail as we hugged. When Katie drove me to the airport he didn't stand out in the road, waving me out of sight as he always used to do. I'll need all my strength not to hurry back for him.

### 20 July, Namibia

Have driven north with Günter Kock, a generous and highly energized stevedore who handles the ships at the Walvis Bay docks. Our task now: to track down Kwazarane again.

**Dusk:** this time she's turned up in the settlement of Omungunda, a little behind Onyuva. I jumped out of the vehicle, seeing her, but she'd already guessed it was me. She even got my name right – sort of.

'Benadiss!' She hung herself around a goat-chewed tree, arranging her limbs, probably wondering if I'd brought her a present. I had. She'd asked last time for a bit of material for her father's skirt. I'd spent hours looking for some, in the end buying horrendously expensive suit fabric. And all because the colour the Himba prize is black.

This is a settlement of only four huts and no sacred fire. It's a temporary outpost. By the look of the freshly smoothed-over cowpat walls the family has only just arrived, drawn this way by better grazing. Now Günter's Toyota has left, and with my new translator, Siggi, I am camped ignominiously amidst ever-bleating goats, which have unfortunately decided to settle in our dry riverbed.

### 21 July

Kwazarane drifted into my camp while I was enjoying some cornflakes. I gave her some, but she only fished at hers unenthusiastically, then skipped away to deal with the goats.

Went with Siggi to Kwazarane's uncle, Wapenga, and discussed my intentions here so as to avoid any problems. Normally he's an easy-going man and has a beautiful, infectious laugh, but today his face suddenly tightened. 'You are trying to take her away to marry?'

I said, quickly, 'No, no. I assure you.'

'Take her, take her please!' That wheezing laugh again, this time totally unrestrained.

In the background, K dressed up as I've never seen her. On her head, replacing the scrap of black plastic binliner, is the women's *erembe* head-dress. Made of soft crests of leather it in theory indicates she's now married anyway – though I think actually she's only promised. Hanging down her chest is the white shell, and down her back a woven metal-link plate. The iron for this is beaten from wire stolen – in what has become a tradition – from a farmer's fence; the copper in her thick collar, however, is customarily acquired from telephone wires. Each piece of jewellery defines her status in the tribe, welds her into the collective whole.

I asked Siggi if he had ever had a Himba girlfriend. He had, he said, but like all Herero boys he found her ochre greasepaint was ruining all his clothes.

Another scorching day. Somewhere far away, more distant than any other sound we can hear, Kwazarane calling to her goats: 'Agg, Agg ... .' Down at the waterhole, two unmarried girlfriends of hers are watering cows. One girl, Vecha-keenya [Vet-cha-keen-ya], vivacious, and aged about fifteen. The other, Waze-ara [Wa-thee-a-ra], walks erect and in the refined manner you'd expect of a Victorian lady, though she's about fourteen and also appears pregnant. They were teasing two young men who were busy tipping buckets of water into a tree-trunk trough. Cows still waiting their turn to drink were kept at bay by a barrage of stones chucked by a line of very small children.

### 22 July

In the morning, the sound of distressed kid goats being divided from their mothers for the day by the deft hands of Kwazarane. Bushes around us shuddering, being got at by the departing goat adults. The clatter of their feet on the riverbed gravels. Occasionally, the crying of Chaweza [Cha-we-tha], who's been flicked in the ear by Kwazarane. She's barely more than a toddler and wears only a little coxcomb of hair, but is already expected to play her part in the herding. So is Komogunjera, the young girl with the two front plaits. She keeps releasing a poignant 'Heeeeee!' sigh of tragedy – probably also one of Kwazarane's torture victims.

### 23 July

Kwazarane has turned up for her breakfast. She's discovered she likes muesli. She's presently lounging on my sleeping bag, chomping through her second bowlful.

*An itinerant healer at Onyuva examining the intestines of a goat to divine the cause of a woman's sickness. Labelled simply 'witch doctors' by our Christian culture, these healers continue to survive in the fast-eroding world of the Himba, not only by drawing on their vast fund of herbal knowledge but also in their traditional role as spiritual interpreters and even what we might call psychiatrists.*

As the sun rose the colours evaporated off the land, to condense once again only when the sun is sinking into the dust layers of the horizon.

Ka-ada is a warm, dear woman with twinkly eyes; she sits with me, patiently untangling this knotty language. She is unflappable, unshockable. She makes me think of my dear old Mum. 'How far that little candle …'

Am I strong enough to be alone in this desert? I've built a tough shell around me to keep out painful thoughts of home – thoughts of Dad out there, of Mum not out there. And I know I have come to the Himba not only to empty myself a little of Western thinking, my usual preparation for an expedition, but also so that, in coming months, I can tell myself I'm not all alone – that this desert margin is a home for people, people who would welcome me in if I needed it.

### 24 July

Kwazarane in my camp again. Never steals or asks, but consumes whatever given. Already seems to be getting podgy – she had to loosen her goatskin belt. I conversed a little in Himba, a language composed of innumerable and ever-changing prefixes beginning mostly with 'o'. At her insistence I'm trying to teach her to count from one to ten in English. She watches my lips, then tries it, but always gets stuck on four. Blames the problem on her missing bottom four incisors. They were knocked out, as tradition demands for both males and females, when 'a man with a mallet came around'. Actually, it's considered that you can't even pronounce the Himba language correctly until the teeth are removed – but I'm not quite *that* dedicated to linguistics.

*Later:* Siggi gave a present to Kwazarane, his bouncy ball. When he first chucked it to her she ducked, thinking it was a rock. It took her ten minutes to learn to stand her ground. However, in the space of one day she's now become astoundingly accurate, her sense of distance perfect.

### 25 July

Went looking for stray goats with Kwazarane. We looked out from a little hill. 'Ongombo,' 'goat', she said, leaning her arm heavily on me as she pointed. She devoured another tin of meat. Scampered downhill together. Halfway to the bottom, she stopped and bent down to pick up a small pebble. She faced me, and put it behind her back. I understood I had to choose which hand it was in. This wasn't difficult – her face is always easy to read. Soon she resorted to cheating, slotting the stone in her mouth and lodging it in the hole between her lower teeth. She giggled most of the way home, popping out the stone with her tongue. She stopped to gather firewood – plonking a long branch on her head and walking on. Then stopped again to rip open a broken old tree, chewing a stick to make it into a brush, and dipping it into the tree's heart. To my surprise, she then wiped the stick across my lips – like an older sister helping a child to feed. Honey. But just as I was about to ask for more she called me away: the sun was dropping fast.

Kwazarane didn't come over to our camp this evening, nor was she out there in the dark calling to escapee goats. Went to investigate and found her in her hut entrance, dropped off to sleep. Curled up, hugging the bouncy ball tight.

### 26 July

Most of the day I was with Ka-ada, still trying to learn what language I could.

Meanwhile, at Onyuva, a woman is sick. The spiritual healer – 'witch doctor' to some – is already bent over the carcass of a slaughtered goat, reading its entrails. He does this divination with great aplomb, clearing away spectators so that I can film him better. A sense of showmanship, a mastery of herbal knowledge and the distance this wanderer keeps from the community allow him respect. As Jesus pointed out, a prophet is never welcome in his own home.

## *27 July*

There are plans to build a dam at Epupa, a hydro-electric project to harness the Kunene, flooding Himba ancestral graves and land.

Ironically, even if this prestigious non-starter doesn't materialize the land won't necessarily continue to be safe in the hands of the Himba either. Whereas the original inhabitants of Southern Africa, the usurped hunter-gatherer 'Bushmen', traditionally used all resources with caution – they never, for example, destroyed a beehive when extracting honey – the Himba and the rest were held in check only by the harshness of the land on which they depended. And now medical clinics, cash from tourists and cash from their cows have released them. They are beginning to settle longer. On my recce of the Kunene I noticed that they were burning the river banks and planting maize – a catastrophe for such a narrow corridor of life. That doesn't mean the Himba are to blame – it's we, not they, who bear the responsibility for the problems we've set in motion.

Kwazarane took me for a walk behind the southern plateau. For her, it was a search for a lost goat. For me it was another vital step towards gaining her trust – and with that, a step to understanding her life, this land. She walked way ahead, working over the stone-littered slopes, sweeping through dry, tall grasses. Her little cousin Chaweza, tried to keep pace, the grasses up to her neck. Seed pods rattled. Kwazarane would stop at a high ridge and look out, the low winter sun shining on her shoulders, arms – all the curves. She was dressed up in her heavy iron belt, an extra skin apron and tail, her conch shell, her head crest. We walked and walked, tucking into a high valley I'd never seen. Chaweza was given no help, was just expected to take it – the heat, the adult stride. At last Kwazarane sat herself down heavily – the weight of all that iron – and waited for me to offer my tin of luncheon meat. I was grateful for the trust she was showing me. We were alone out here with the occasional gazelle, the rocks, the stiff yellow grasses. Sometimes a locust showed itself, passing with one giant, clumsy hop. A thin black and white snake eased out from under our rock and, seeing us, eased back into it again. We sat, catching our breath, silent in a silent land.

After a while Kwazarane signalled that it was time for me to go back. I pretended to cry, and she giggled slightly – but was firm. I hoiked Chaweza on to my back and lugged her home. I'm so aware that any day Kwazarane may be gone. Her loyalties are not to me – and nor should they be. One day her father will summon her, and she'll be off out of this settlement, and on to the next task of his. Perhaps marriage.

## 28 July

Day after burning day sitting under trees hung with goat's meat – a leg, a head. Often I have only the pied crows for company as I learn the Himba language from Ka-ada – it'll help when I come through with my camels – or do tasks with Kwazarane. Sometimes I use my time to test my expedition equipment. Because of the innate character of much of this desert – blinding fogs, shifting dunes – using a sextant or map and compass to navigate is often impossible and the BBC insists on me taking a GPS [global positioning system], a little gadget which positions you almost exactly. I'll use it as a last resort only – I regard most Western intrusions with suspicion. However, I can't help but admire the solar panels – the quiet way they get on with their job, soaking up the sun's energy. Their task is to recharge my camera batteries, though it remains to be seen whether Nelson will allow them to fit either side of his hump.

The only other person around to teach me today is Komogunjera – a thoughtful but manipulative child. She enjoys looking at the world through the two plaits trailing over her face. Soon she will have her first [monthly] period and go to her father to have her hair fashioned into a curtain of plaits to drape over her face. I asked her, partly in sign language, if she was worried about having her lower front teeth knocked out, something that will also happen shortly. She indicated she wouldn't cry. That's maybe true, and the Himbas do apparently chew herbal leaves to numb and disinfect the jaw – but the adults present moaned just thinking about it. Certainly there's an acceptance here of what life brings. Imagine being a Western child waiting for the day when you'll have four of your teeth bashed out: the dread would cloud your whole childhood.

## 29 July

Wapenga is pounding snuff on a stone. Ka-ada is busily brewing beer from a fermented small seed. Siggi has gone, sent by me to Okandjombo where K's headman father lives, to tell them a white man will one day come through this way with strange humped animals and could he lend guidance if they happen to hear of me approaching.

There's no doubt I've begun to slow down to the motion of these people, and I think that will be the key to my success both with the desert and with those desert quadrupeds, the camels. The irony is, though I say I distrust Western technology as a tool of exploration, that camels aren't actually indigenous to Africa

*Overleaf: Chaweza, though little more than a toddler, is expected to take her part in daily tasks, here the female role of goat- and sheep-herd.*

either – they evolved in North America and, since their spread into Asia, have been brought across to North Africa and then further and further down the continent by man.

*Night-time:* the whole family is sitting around the fire in a screaming cold wind. We've been playing that game in which you hide a stone in one of your hands, notching our scores up in the dust. It acts as a binding mechanism . We have no common language, but in the search for the stone we search each other's eyes in the firelight, reading them before darting to the chosen hand.

### 30 July

The notorious bergwind blows in hot gusts from the east, wrapping me and my camp in fine dust. Took my shoes – falling to bits from the stony ground – to Kwazarane's hut to have them stitched up.

*Midday:* Kwazarane has gone. The stitching was the last thing she will do for me. A man – bold, silent – came trotting up on a fine horse, a bridle fashioned gloriously from strips cut from car tyres. Kwazarane dressed herself up and began arranging her things, carefully stuffing the bouncy ball in with her goatskins. Komogunjera, the small girl, brought a mule for her to ride off with.

The man spoke some English. 'Kwazarane go now.'

'She's *going*? Today? Now? When's she back?'

'Not come back. She has heavy heart. Heavy. You friend her. Heavy. Thank you. Sorry.'

I thought: 'She may well be sorry, but she isn't showing it.' I needed a goodbye, a conclusion. She was just standing ready to go, her little bag already on the mule, the bouncy ball waiting for her.

When the young man ordered, she did come up to say goodbye. She smiled a second, then looked away, and I could see now she was feeling guilty. I said, struggling for Himba words, 'You here, when I come back with camels?'

Silence.

'Yes, she wait you,' the boy said, kindly.

But she will not be waiting for me. She hasn't the power to choose, whether she wants it or not. I smiled and thanked her, making the best of it.

She trotted off, and I ran alongside for a while. 'Bye, bye,' I said in English, and she smiled properly at me. It was enough: I felt much better then.

### 31 July

Ka-ada undoubtedly sorry for me. She has come over to my camp, and sits teaching me new words. Wapenga is asleep in his hut, his head resting on a little wooden pillow block. Soon Ka-ada will be quietly making yoghurt – swish, swish. In this desert it is as calming a sound as a trickling fountain.

*Midday:* Ka-ada and I watched a goat give birth to triplets. Suddenly out of the sleepy heat came a low, mechanical noise. Chaweza and the other children skipped about. They screamed, '*Ondera*!' The word for bird. Wapenga got out his staff and jokingly brandished it at the sky. It was a plane, coming in very low. This could only be André Schoeman looking for me. He'll have dropped a message in one of the Himba settlements, giving me a rendezvous point. My stay here is almost over.

### 1 August

I took a last walk, surveying the stones, thinking through the future, wondering if I'll make it through here with the camels. I do feel stronger, deep down inside. Kwazarane and her family have been my guides, my way into this countryside of rocks. I am better prepared. My heart now feels more at home in the Namib.

But now I've got to step back a while into the West – timetables, priority lists, maps. Take a deep breath …

# 3

# NELSON, TOP CAMEL

*6 August*

Back to Windhoek. The Namibian press full of stories about 'the camel man'. Government showing signs of getting scared – last-minute nerves. Pressure on me via Tommy Hall to have vehicle back-up 'which for safety's sake should mean two vehicles and two drivers in each vehicle'. The British press I was intending to boycott as a result of the *Daily Telegraph*'s slip into fantasy last time. 'Benedict Allen, real live Indiana Jones, or just a day dreamer?' However, I've relented, deciding on one full interview with their rivals *The Times*.

*8 August*

Through the night by bus, down into South Africa, nearer and nearer to the three unfortunate camel individuals whose hearts I must win. From Upington, whisked north into the Kalahari by Willie Knoesen's brother (or uncle?) – and his pastor, who was on a hunting trip and looked like an Afrikaner secret policeman. At last across the salt pan, the road twisting up into that smooth boulder hill hemmed by the ochre band of the Kalahari, the largest continuous area of sand in the world. Then the farm below, a little green patch among the family's 35,000 hectares of dust – looks like hardly a tree otherwise on it.

I settled into the bungalow where Mrs Knoesen has lodged me and had a wel-

*Having a quiet word with Jan, the camel whose health and violent outbursts were to cause me the most heart-ache. Both he and Andries took their lead from Top Camel, Nelson, who here looks away, unimpressed.*

coming cup of tea in the kitchen, the doorstep of which is occupied by a roll of cloth which serves to keep out snakes. The farm is snuggled among the black hills, an Eden of orange trees and flowering shrubs all fed by bathwater. It is watched over by guard-dog Stefi, who alone now in South Africa I hope, still runs his life along apartheid lines: he attacks those that are known here as 'blacks' and 'coloureds' – the mix-blooded farm workers – and worships 'whites'. Ostriches charge in flocks, their wide, gullible eyes steady; windmill blades spin, weaver birds flit.

All afternoon I watched Willie Knoesen's entire fleet of camels – ten or more of them – and the way the workers trained them with a whip. I have the men's help for a week. Then I'm alone – two more weeks in which to master animals that can kick in all directions and use their knees as well. Knoesen came over. 'They will be watching you,' he said. 'Seeing if you are weak. And *where* you are weak.'

As the heat rose, the farm workers curled their balaclavas up off their faces. They walked about in the kraal like *Lawrence of Arabia* film extras, herding a set of neurotic baby camels and – rather more gingerly, I thought – manoeuvring mine.

The key to my journey is mastering Nelson, the leader. He must learn to see me as Top Camel. And to this end I've brought him some carrots – a tip from London Zoo.

Too old to learn? Willie K claims Nelson is only eleven. This may be true, and his greying coat deceptive. But Nelson has seen the world – he has that knowing look. He also gnashes his teeth, making the enamel squeak. In his winter coat, he's like a teddy bear with an unlucky past.

Skerpioen, the second camel, is contrary and irritating. His presence also seems to annoy Nelson. That leaves Jan, who is young and, thankfully, straightforward.

### 9 August

With the farm hands' help I sat Skerpioen and Nelson down and began saddling them and two young camels being trained: Isak and the famous Andries – a happy, pre-adolescent little creature who's tipped as a future star. During the saddling, Nelson sat grizzling, breathing hoarsely and sending a cascade of warm spittle from his open mouth. He showed his yellow canines, threatening to bite – that huge jaw that would so comfortably fit around my throat. It isn't an idle threat. 'Bite from camel,' says one entry in the death columns of the Windhoek Archives from a hundred years ago, when Namibia was patrolled by the German Camel Corps. 'In the neck,' it explains – or some other such words of equally admirable succinctness. But the most dangerous weapon in the camel's formidable arsenal is the brisket, the cartilaginous pad on its chest. Normally used to bear the weight of the sitting camel, it also crushes predators once they've been kicked over.

The camels that we'd left behind began mooing like cows, a lonely, imploring call which wrings even the human heart. We sat Nelson, Skerpioen and the two young ones down – eventually – and checked girth straps and reins. Andries, the future star, was the first to be mounted. It took about two seconds, maybe three, for him to throw his rider off.

I was next to mount. Nelson eyed me, daring me to get on him. I climbed aboard – it felt like a ship. Nelson surged to his feet, hoping to surprise me. Too late: I was on.

Knoesen had said that by the end of today I mustn't have been forced off by Nelson. 'If you're thrown, you must get straight back on. Right away, even if your leg's broken. Nelson must know he hasn't won.' But very soon I was in agony. Every internal organ of mine seemed to have been mashed. The workers said he was deliberately giving me a rough ride.

For the next five hours – that is, all the time we were heading away from the farm – Nelson's efforts were concentrated on getting back home. He seemed to be systematically working out a way to get rid of me. He sat down without warning; he tried to wipe me off him on a useful tree branch; he tried stopping at random; he tried heading off into the veld – anywhere, anything. All the time the workers were kept busy riding behind, blocking Nelson's exit with a whip.

Finally, we decided to turn home. And Nelson ran hell for leather, a jarring trot which hammered my poor joints until I wanted to scream.

*Evening:* the guard-dog, Stefi, is sitting with me as I lie in a heap, my body in shock.

### 10 August

Woke this morning feeling terrible – my legs as stiff as crutches. Can't face another full day with Nelson. I'll ride one of the others.

*Evening:* Skerpioen gave me a hard, bouncy ride. Within an hour I had to swap to Jan, and he was worse. And so I ended up being persecuted by Nelson again.

*Overleaf:* Twilight at Koppieskraal, north of Upington, South Africa. The Knoesen family's farm is perched on the edge of the Kalahari, the largest continuous expanse of sand in the world, and, until the early 1950s, the police kept camels with which to patrol it.

I planned to go beyond the black hills, past those boulders balanced improbably on each other and on towards the ochre dunes. I wanted to know as soon as possible: could these camels be made to climb sand slopes?

Nelson is set in his ways, single-minded and outrageous. When Skerpioen bumps into him, he lets out a grunt of displeasure and bumps him back. He also likes to walk at half a beat slower than Skerpioen, and mutters when Skerpioen jerks him forward. Nelson can't be bothered to do things that don't suit him – for example, it's a chore for him to sit down, to let me off at the end of the day, so he doesn't. He wants an easy life. I have to make sure he knows that obeying me is the easiest way to attain one.

**11 August**
**Dawn:** the dunes are a worry, but so are the stones. My hard training programme (I rode 40 kilometres yesterday) is already ripping their feet to bits. Skerpioen's back right foot is red and raw on the outer toe. Nelson's also starting to bleed. I splashed Stockholm tar on the toenails, using ostrich feathers. It will help seal them, but won't solve the problem. Willie Knoesen and I are talking of making some boots. Another possibility is to use a glue to harden the nails. But the pads too are wearing down.

**Late afternoon:** I don't want to see another camel today. I'm writing this up in the hills around the farm. Up here, the rocks are stacked as if by giants at play. Among them scamper rockrabbits [hyraxes, dassies]. Their sentries are sitting and staring at me, hunched on the battlements ready to bark warnings. They look like overgrown guinea pigs, but are actually ungulates or hoofed creatures. Their nearest relative could be the elephant; their front teeth are miniature tusks, and like the elephant they have blunt plates for nails. Moist pads on their feet serve as suction pads as they hop about the black burnished walls of this natural castle.

Explorers have sought such a place for a century. In 1886 G.A. Farini published an account of his journey through the Kalahari in which he found a ruined city, much of the remains 'like the Chinese Wall after an earthquake'. He traced the ruins for nearly 2 kilometres and claimed to have found an altar, the fluted base of which was still distinctly visible. 'The masonry was of a cyclopean character,' he told the RGS [Royal Geographical Society]. 'Here and there the gigantic square blocks still stood on each other.' Michael Main's book on the Kalahari suggests that by the 1960s three expeditions a year were setting out to find the city. It has never been found. One researcher, A.J. Clement, gives an explanation. Farini was born William Leonard Hunt. He was a showman and entertainer who crossed the Niagara Falls by tightrope at the age of twenty-five. The lost city? Just another bit of showmanship.

But this tranquil place is like a citadel to me, defending me against unwanted camel thoughts.

## 12 August

I must rest the camels' feet so I took out just Jan and Nelson, walking them about the farm by myself. Jan is young, maybe five years old, and he enjoys physical contact, and nuzzles me more than the other two. Especially when I try to get him to do things he doesn't want he puts his face to mine: 'Dear, dear, Benedict,' he seems to say. 'We are all so fond of you … ' Nelson too is not above pleading. He comes up behind you and suddenly you find soft but bristly lips against your cheek.

## 13 August

Lonely, frustrating day. Not helped by the arrival of my very own saddles. Specially fashioned for me along the lines of those used by the German pioneers, they are a reminder that this isn't a game.

I'm alone here – workers' day off – and the camels won't leave their field to come with me. Bribes useless. Nelson ate all my special carrots, apparently in a single mouthful, while I was talking to Jan.

By sunset I was almost in tears. I sat down and watched the sands burn red with the last light, then darken to a molten fire. Three eland poised on a dune ridge, then bolted, melting away in the glowing veld. A bat-eared fox pattered through the sands, directing its ears to the ground, listening for subterranean movement – the worms and mice that it adores.

## 14 August

My plan had been to get right away from the farm for a few days. Headed off with the three camels, me riding Nelson, Skerpioen's rein held in my right hand, and Jan (the farm hand) riding behind with Jan the camel. We trotted right across the pan and on into the veld. Nelson became more and more disagreeable as the farmlands he knew disappeared.

Finally we reached the veld, 25 kilometres away. We'll be camping for three days, and when Nelson realized we weren't heading home he roared continuously, and would do nothing but go round and round in circles.

We lit a fire, and now it's night. A bushy tail has just swept by in the dimness – the phantom presence of a Cape fox. Not an insect to be heard – absolute silence except for the whooping of the fire.

I've decided that tomorrow I'd better let the worker, Jan, go back to the farm when Knoesen comes along to check on us. I'll be stuck out here, alone with these brutes, but it's the only way. I have to be able to cope by myself. The problem isn't just that they are wearing me down. None of the equipment is up to Nelson's standard. He bent a metal halter ring yesterday, and now his saddle. Or rather I have – all my strength pushing against Nelson's almighty neck.

Should I resort to using the camels' nose pegs? These pegs, which have already been placed in Jan's and Nelson's nostrils, are designed to be attached to strings and used to steer the camel's head. But the camel's nose is sensitive, the method harsh. I am still hoping that the reins are enough. Robyn Davidson, an Australian who took camels across Western Australia, said, 'Because camels' necks are so strong the nose-line is essential for riding a camel. It is almost impossible to control them with just a halter, unless you have superhuman strength.' I am in fact strong enough to yank Nelson's head right back. It does little good. He thrashes, his boiling mouth like a cauldron. But I don't want to use whips, I don't want to use nose pegs. Not until I'm desperate. Next week?

**15 August**

Near disaster. It's now night. I'm lying alone by the campfire, left hand bleeding. Camels somewhere far off, roaming free.

I was on foot, leading them – or rather herding them – when suddenly they ran, making me sprint behind. Soon I was flying on the end of a training lead. All my sleeping gear and food was strapped on them. I was wearing only a tee-shirt and thin trousers and the sun was almost touching the horizon. A winter frost was likely. My only hope of catching the creatures was to use their speed to swing me out in an arc and head them off. I was propelled faster than any Olympic sprinter by the combined force of three camels. When my legs couldn't keep up, I was hurled: over bushes, over hillocks. Some primeval instinct told me I mustn't let go. My hands were slashed, the rope sawed deep into the palm of my hand. I couldn't hold on any longer. The camels galloped away, triumphant.

At last light, I managed to corner them against a fence. Stood gasping, hardly able to issue the orders for the camels to sit. 'Koes!' I wheezed. Oddly enough, they all obeyed immediately. They looked extremely guilty. I took off the saddles and gear, and gathered firewood in the near dark. Nelson then set out at a smart

*A rockrabbit, hyrax or dassie (Procavia capensis), poised between the rocks above Koppieskraal. Resembling in places the ruins of walls and battlements, these stacked angular blocks might be the origin of the tales of the Lost City of the Kalahari.*

pace, the others tagging behind like members of his platoon.

### *16 August*

I tried every combination under the sun: riding each camel in turn, then positioning them differently in the caravan – to the left and right, and in front and behind of each other. I became more and more forceful, sometimes having to use the whip. Nelson – searching for that elusive 'easy life' – responded, but angrily. Skerpioen – free spirit, stubborn, brilliant (or stupid) – decided that today he would rather not respond. N got more and more irate with him. I could see Skerpioen was getting scared – of Nelson, not me. Yet still he wouldn't budge. Nelson really did want to do what I wanted, I'm sure.

Finally, I took Skerpioen away and hid him behind a bush, hobbling him tight. I half-hoped a cobra would get him there. Then I returned to where I'd hobbled Nelson and Jan. I tied Jan to Nelson and gathered Nelson's reins. Nelson performed his classic manoeuvre – jumping up just as I was trying to mount him. But today the speed with which he did this took me by surprise. It was also a surprise to Jan, who reared, throwing Nelson into disarray. I hung on – it's a long way to fly from a camel to the ground. Nelson tossed me again, doing the job properly this time. I came down heavily on my left foot, feeling something snap.

One of the first things I did, as I lay in the dirt, was to move my foot to see if it was broken. No – not this time.

My vulnerability in the desert is suddenly very palpable. Without the camels, I'm stranded. At last I was able to climb back on board Nelson. That took some nerve – him roaring, my ankle screaming. For the last two hours I've been soaking my foot in the sheep trough to stop the swelling and to dim the pain. Such is my schedule, I can't let this injury slow me even by one day.

Another thing: because I was limping I was slow undoing the halters at the end of the day. Jan became restless, seeing the others drift away to graze. He charged over to them – making sure I was in the way, raising his knees as he trotted, really going for me. I was lucky to be caught by only one knee – a thump in the chest like a mallet blow. Maybe Jan isn't quite as straightforward as I used to think.

***Night-time:*** the reassuring clinking of the metal wind pump. I must learn to think more like a camel – exploiting weakness, and using more cunning than logic. Two things I'm constantly aware of. First, Nelson has an uncanny sense of direction. He always knows where home is. This means that if I need to recover control of the camels, I should turn him homeward. And second, the camels are very insecure when not together. Thus one camel can always be left free. He will always follow – even Nelson will. In effect, I have to master only two camels.

### 17 August

A restless night. Woke to find my heart pounding. Not a sound in the veld otherwise. No crickets, no cicadas. Wish someone would appear out of the blue and say, 'I'm really, really sorry, Benedict. The expedition's off. The government no longer wants to take the risk.'

### 18 August

Back at the farm, the battle is joined. The camels now know I'm a threat to their pleasant life grazing in the veld, and every day they fight harder. I mustn't be sentimental about these tough desert animals. I won't use nose pegs, though.

Today, when Jan began to push Nelson off course, I gave him a whack. Soon I had to do it again, and I winced. But the next thing Jan was eating my stick up, savouring the juicy bark.

Tried to take Nelson and Jan out without Skerpioen. This did not go down well. Mrs Knoesen consoled me with a cup of tea and some good old Afrikaner resilience: 'Things must be made bad before they get better.' I didn't want to leave the comfort of her kitchen ever again – the singing kettle, the tablecloth.

### 19 August

I keep checking the date, nervously counting the days. Today Jan kicked a BBC camera out of my hand. This camel that I once found so sweet – and who is still so endearing with his little nuzzles – has been blocking Nelson's attempts to obey me. There's no longer any doubt. He winds his long, supple neck around Nelson's, entreating him not to listen to me. As for Skerpioen, I now understand the origin of his name. Not because he kicks, but because he has an insect's cold, functional heart.

### 20 August

This is a war of attrition and I'm wearing down faster than they are. You only have to look at my legs, now bruised blue from my groin to my ankles.

Mrs Knoesen puts aside her tasks – cooking rusks, cutting biltong [dried meat] – and makes me another restorative pot of tea. Afterwards, still exhausted, I go outside to do battle again.

In the sun I lean against the camels, feeling sad and exploited by them. The camels stand out in the sun leaning against me, hardly caring. Today old Mr

*Assembling a camel team from scratch. In three weeks, ready or not, a lorry would take us away and we'd be launched out into desert. My injuries mounted as I fought a war of attrition with Nelson, who here tries to prevent me from leading the others across a salt pan.*

Knoesen, Willie Knoesen's father, emerged from the veranda where he often watches my sorry progress. He walked over in his boots, the only taut muscles now those of his iron jaw, and the hand on his big leather whip. Slashes out at the camels – it was the movement, suddenly, of a youth again. The camels stepped forward, in shock. The old man staggered after them again and again. How the Boers lost the war against the British, heaven knows.

Ten days to go. Nose peg time? Willie Knoesen, who turns out to have a really kind heart, agrees with me – there must be another way. 'Nelson has a powerful neck. He'll turn round and create trouble.' Yet I don't feel Nelson would bite me, not now. My reluctance to use the stick has paid off with him. We have, I think, the beginnings of mutual respect – like the sort between old enemy soldiers.

### 21 August

Can hardly write. Don't ask …

I was riding Jan when he suddenly got frightened by some loose saddle padding which flapped down his side. Tossed and tossed me. My knuckles – already in a bad enough state – were ground against the saddle's front bar. But I couldn't face

*A moment later: Nelson mounts a strike and wins yet again. My ultimate goal was to master him and become Top Camel myself.*

the pain of a plunge on to my sprained ankle. I held on. Finally, Jan did calm down. But now only one of my knuckles isn't skinned, and my wrist is very bad. It looks like an artificial one.

Nelson broke another halter. That's one BBC camera, three halters, one saddle.

***Evening:*** Tommy Hall rang. Scary – a voice from the world out there that's waiting for me. Security arrangements finalized. Permission has been secured for Adrian to join the Namdeb security people to take photos in the Sperrgebiet diamond area. Tommy tells me today's newspaper headlines: 'Explorer must conquer camels before the desert.'

As I've arranged, the Namdeb horse transport lorry will collect the camels from here and transport them (and me) to near Oranjemund, the closed diamond mining town at the Orange River mouth. Jan Coetzer from security has very kindly agreed to erect a pen for them at Hohenfels, right on the river bank, with a hessian screen so they'll be sheltered from the driving mist. My hope is that they'll acclimatize to the damp coast as we gently walk them downriver to Oranjemund and the start of the Sperrgebiet the next day. I also have a kraal organized at the other side of the Sperrgebiet, at the isolated town of Lüderitz, with Gary, an off-shore diamond diver and devoted horseman. Should we then get from there through the Namib-Naukluft Park to the next settlement, Walvis Bay, that town's riding stables will also take the camels in. From there on, through the rocky north, I'll be alone, but Günter Kock, with Woker Freight Transport, will help with supply drops. Rather sobering: I've asked Tommy to bring his pistol in case a camel has a bad fall and we have to put it out of its misery.

Many questions from Tommy regarding my expected pace per day (25 kilometres), and the hay, lucerne and horse pellets that have been shipped into our starting point at Oranjemund and to Walvis Bay. Wanted to know about my supplies of veterinary medicine – antibiotics, dressings. He laughed (nervously?) when I said I'd just fallen off. Reality's dawning for him – these are not like his horses. He'll have time to adjust to them through the Sperrgebiet, when we have to have the diamond security people watching over us anyway, but now Tommy's saying that the government definitely want a vehicle to keep an eye on me from Lüderitz through the closed Namib-Naukluft Park. To my protests, he's saying that taking only one vehicle and driver is already a compromise – even a big risk. How do you drag it out if it gets stuck? My answer: you don't. Just leave the thing to die horribly. But now even the experts are seriously worried and I've conceded.

Another kick in the ribs from Jan. And I woke last night to find a strange arm lying across me. It was mine – heavy with bruising and new muscle.

## *22 August*

First European swallows arriving now, arching around farm sheds, spinning, spiralling. With help from a farm hand I walked out to the south, yanking the camels behind me – three against one. Whole hills have been smothered by shifting sands there. Dark, brittle stones choked by sepias, angry reds, burnt umbers. Waves of gentle sands splash down on to rocks, lying like forgotten beaches. And out here in the middle of it all: me, suffering trial by camel.

The farm workers came by, rounding up sheep with a few of the young camels. I watched Andries, the youthful creature that threw a worker so effortlessly two weeks ago. Extremely playful, but brilliant. Today he was even obeying at times.

He was weaving around the sheep flock – intuitive, gentle. I trudged up on foot with Nelson and my pitiful team, and on a whim asked to swap Andries, for a moment, with Skerpioen.

You could notice the change even before we set off together. Young Andries instinctively took his lead from Nelson, and now Jan suddenly found he didn't have an accomplice any more. We walked together along a track for half an hour. It was all I needed. In that time we had only one problem – when Nelson moved left, to be on his favourite side of the track, he knocked Andries into a gate-post.

I came back to the farm with a spring in my stride – despite my bandages. Now it's night, and I'm thinking: 'Can I sack Skerpioen?' But Andries would only be able to carry 55 kilograms. Worse, he has no bodily food reserves to cope with the desert – his hump turns out to be no more than a mound of baby fluff.

'It's a risk,' says Knoesen.

It is, but taking Skerpioen is also a risk. At the very least Andries isn't as strong – he can be dragged with a lead rein more easily.

### 23 August

With Willie shunting from behind with his car, I got the three camels out on to the pan. I was riding Nelson, with Jan to my right, Andries to my left.

Then Willie's 4 x 4 swung round, back towards home. It felt magnificent: peace and, with it, freedom. Nelson looked agreeably around, letting me take him further and further from the farm. We were like a ship on a sea; an orderly crew working together and actually going places.

Far, far away, the moans of Skerpioen. Heart-rending cries of agonized betrayal. But with Andries, who now hero-worships Nelson, I have a team.

We walked home across the pan. A whole day together, and no blood shed.

### 30 August

My last day. I went up to Knoesen, who was washing his penknife after using it to castrate Andries' ex-classmates. 'You think I've made the right decision?'

He replied, 'I doubt if Andries will make the journey.'

I said I was actually hoping for a word of encouragement.

He said that if I took it slowly, allowed him to eat as we walked, maybe he'd be all right.

'There must be something to eat out there. Otherwise there'd be gemsbok [oryx] skeletons everywhere.'

'But there are,' I murmured, picturing the bones of this ultimate desert survivor sticking out of the sand. I went off to introduce horse pellets to Andries. Already I've been weaning Nelson and Jan on to them, preparing their stomachs for the lack of natural vegetation ahead. Next I assembled the camels and my equipment. Food I'd buy in Oranjemund, but with some ceremony I checked off the rest of my kit: the medical supplies – featuring extremely impressive-looking syringe needles to be jabbed into camel upper thighs as instructed by Knoesen's farm vet – a sleeping bag, sleeping mat, mini-tent, a little gas stove, my long-bladed throwing knife for cutting reins in an emergency, spare girth straps, ropes and reins, a sewing kit, boots, video and still cameras, livestock importation certificates, maps, compasses, GPS, thin clothes for the heat (long-sleeve shirts to lessen dehydration) and thick clothes for the fogs. All this and more I placed into huge black canvas bags tightly strapped atop the saddles, along with one 25-litre water container each. Finally, I tied the BBC solar panels either side of Nelson's hump. A perfect fit.

### 2 September

Mayhem as the camels were dragged by rope into the horse transporter. Nelson sat down in protest, and had to be slid aboard on a bed of sand.

Off we went, dust ballooning behind us, bronze crags coming and going, the lone silver stumpy quiver trees, the gravel horizons. Dark came, and at a petrol station the two drivers got out to check the tyres. I got out and checked the camels: their bewildered faces peered out into the neon-lit forecourt. The camels' legs were shaking and Jan had a slash on his rear left thigh. But what struck me more than anything was that for the first time the camels were looking to me for help, as children do to a parent. Their eyes seemed to be pleading.

Then onward, cars flashing by in the night, until ahead we saw the sunrise seep through the mist of the Orange River. On the far bank lay Namibia. From here, the starting point of the journey, there would be no substantial running water until Angola, the other end of the country. My target, the Kunene River, was three and a half months' walk away.

We drove through the South African border post, across the Sir Ernest Oppenheimer Bridge, through tangerine mist that was soaking up the first sun's rays, to report to the security gate at the entrance to Oranjemund.

Then followed the river inland – this great river which millions of years ago brought the diamonds from the interior, unloading them at the river mouth for the currents to scatter them north up the Skeleton Coast.

A kraal stood waiting, just as Jan Coetzer had promised, specially screened with hessian. Tommy Hall, alerted by security, bounded up for his first glimpse of Nelson, Jan and Andries. His eyes half analytical, half wondrous – a rare combination. With him was Dr Dieter Noli, an archaeologist and historian who has special permission to work in the Sperrgebiet. And there, thank God, was Adrian, a real ally – face still pale from London, Nikons slung like sacred rocks around his neck. But my mind was on the quaking transportees. The drivers backed up the lorry and we slowly let down the back ramp.

Nelson seemed cowed, reduced to a lamb by a day and a night in a rocking cage. Jan too was strangely quiet. Andries plodded out joyfully, apparently not

*Ready for action: with Nelson at the Orange River, the start of the*
*three-and-a-half-month walk.*

even noticing he'd been moved from the desert to a misty river.

While Tommy introduced himself quietly to the camels, I looked around. This was Hohenfels, a remote frontier post built by German military authorities in 1908. Now, only crumbled brick walls. Those whose unlucky lot it was to be posted here were selected for their stamina and mental stability; apart from the monthly camel patrol they saw no other people. But today I noticed on the dank slopes a delicate pink geranium. A plucky little plant, which occurs in the fog zone of the Orange Valley and nowhere else in the world, it extends its soft tissue flowers, as it was doing now, only in the mildness of winter.

My thoughts turned to Tommy. I was relieved to see that he's well aware of the force he's dealing with – he talks to the camels briskly, taking no nonsense. He is too loud, and pats them as if they are horses, which they hate. But he's also respectful. Nelson threatens him with his teeth in a way he never does now with me. I feel a perverse satisfaction: his great force on my side.

### 3 September

Today we rode the camels downriver, towards the security area enclosing Oranjemund and the Sperrgebiet.

Tommy is extremely unfit, but still impressive – not too proud to watch how I work, adjusting girth straps and reins. His loudness frightens the camels, but they do listen to him. An African fish eagle swung overhead, feral donkeys parted, antelope, mainly fat gemsbok, scattered through the reeds. But for the camels everything was too green and thick after the sticky shrubs of the Kalahari. There were bushes blocking the way, biting flies – and swaying trees. The tree sighs terrified them – trees never grow high enough to do anything much in the Kalahari. By mid-afternoon Nelson and Jan kept looking around to me, wondering why we hadn't yet turned back as we'd always done at lunchtime on the farm. Little do they know: from the time of our departure in two days' time there'll be no home except the northern horizon, the direction in which we'll be heading every day.

But tonight their home is Oranjemund, a town with something of an army compound feel: security checkpoints, ID cards. Signposts issue reminders – your safety belt, your oil change. It adjoins a mining zone of even higher security within the Sperrgebiet. To get in there you walk down a corridor lined with notices of men in jail for diamond theft. Helicopters cruise overhead, video cameras scan. Workers are subjected to x-rays on leaving, but vehicles never come out at all. There are acres of Toyotas, Land Rovers, buses. Fields of tyres – all left out there in the wastelands to drop.

I'd arranged accommodation for the camels at the security dog kennels. Before

I left the compound I went for a closer look at Jan. His lack of interest in the world bothered me. While Nelson was busy staring at the lawn – he'd never seen grass so short, green and flat – and Andries playfully walked about inspecting things, Jan couldn't care less. Nor was he eating the hay and horse pellets. Tommy and I eased one of my horse blankets on to him. He didn't complain – and that worried me more than ever.

### 4 September

Final preparations for tomorrow's departure. My day kicked off with a session for schoolchildren.

'Why's he so angry with us?' a child asked, pointing at Nelson who was roaring at the nearest infant.

'He's always like that,' said Tommy, learning fast.

While Tommy worked with Adrian to oil the saddles I gave the next presentation, this time with slides, over lunch, to Namdeb's senior managers' wives. They made me take off my shirt to show my New Guinea tribal initiation marks. Mid-afternoon another lecture, this to the senior managers – who sat in eerie silence. Many believe I can't pull this trip off – Tommy warned me that they're watching me, judging. The security men and geologists know the Namib and even the huge security officers Berti and Johann say they wouldn't cope. 'We're too fast. Too impatient. If something went wrong, we'd panic and give up.' Yet these men look like professional arm wrestlers. On my reconnaissance visit, when a foaming guard-dog set its sights on me and charged, Johann fearlessly stepped between us. He reduced the beast to a cuddly pup.

Final conference with Tommy, his driver Henog, and Adrian. Security patrols will watch us all the way – theoretically to make sure I'm not feeding diamonds to the camels – and we must also be accompanied through the Sperrgebiet by Tommy's vehicle in case of some (unmentioned) mishap. This first stage will take us to Lüderitz, the old desert-bound port built by the Germans, where Gary has built a special kraal at his stables.

One more thing emerged at our meeting. It turns out that *The Times*, the one paper I trusted, has done an outrageous feature entitled, 'Behave camels – or this man will have you for breakfast.' The article – inspired by the fact that I had to eat my dog in the Amazon – makes the desert sound like the 'Killing Fields' and Nelson like a mobile snack. The piece has now been reproduced in a Namibian newspaper. Farmers out here are judged by how well they maintain their livestock, and apparently there's 'bad feeling' awaiting me in Lüderitz.

# 4

# THE FORBIDDEN ZONE

**5 September**

***Dawn:*** Tommy is simply too overweight to go on Jan, and I've had to allocate Nelson to him. I'll go on the 'boneshaker', Jan, myself. However, not today. Jan still hasn't got over the shock of the journey. He looks stunned, he's off his food. I'll lead him on foot.

*Later:* we began saddling up, Tommy watching as I positioned each camel's padding, tightened their two girth straps. We were off at 11a.m., waving at children and well-wishers as we walked the few hundred metres to the great gate into the Sperrgebiet. Behind us the sound of spitting lawn hoses, ahead land that looked like the dirt remains of a nuclear bomb test site. Some delays while Adrian took his photos, security personnel checked our passes and manhandled the gate, and manic guard-dogs tried to get at us through prison camp fencing. Then we walked through. The gate was closed behind us, and padlocked. This was a strange feeling. We were being locked into an open space, an emptiness that stretched for days and days.

So, I thought, as Tommy got on Nelson and I led off Jan and Andries on foot, this is the Sperrgebiet, the 'prohibited zone'. It was created five months after the

*The inner Security Zone fence at Chameis. During the 'Independence Struggle' it was widely considered a patriotic duty to smuggle out diamonds belonging to the South African-based De Beers company. Now, smugglers operate in sophisticated syndicates with trained carriers. Each package bears a syndicate's name, this encoded so that even the carrier doesn't know for which syndicate, ultimately, the diamonds are destined.*

first diamond was found out here in 1908. The German authorities declared the area under their control, hoping the Sperrgebiet would prevent the fatherland, which had found the cost of suppressing the natives unexpectedly high, losing out on the ensuing diamond rush.

From here, all we could see were gravel and sand flats with clumps of salt bush. In a word, it was dull – we'd been instructed to keep to the security patrol route and there was little of interest along the road other than the horned adders squashed by the security patrol cars.

The day was calm and hot, the coastal mists burning off in the sun. To our left lay the razor-wire fence which marked off the heart of the mining operation. I had been permitted in there, under escort, during my reconnaissance trip. It's like another planet – things happen according to quite different rules. Sand and gravel, which would almost anywhere else be dismissed as 'dirt', are treasured. A fleet of 200 earth-moving vehicles busy themselves carrying it about. A bucket-wheel digger of breathtaking dimensions sprawls over the land, scooping it up. Lorries pass by like beetles under this Martian's extended arm. At the end of that arm a toothed wheel gnaws into the ground, each tooth filling a tonne bucket. Now two-thirds of the ore body on land has been mined, so other vast machines are turning their attention to the sea. They are pushing the coastline back, erecting walls to keep off the waves. But wherever it is that the machines search, the greatest attention is reserved for the bedrock, where the diamonds have settled down through the sediments. There men, at times surveyed by video recorders, work the fissures using hand brushes. They ease out every last piece of grit, then finish up with a vacuum cleaner. In 1987, the year I have figures for, the company recovered 1,019,636 carats in total – a carat being one-fifth of a gram. That's 224 million parts of waste handled for every part diamond.

As the camels settled into the walk – I began to notice occasional movement in the low scrub. Ostriches peeked from far horizons. The ears of black-backed jackals twitched from behind cover. Gazelles were also watching, springbok invisible until their heads turned. The small steenbok, literally 'stone buck', watched a while, then flitted away.

***Night-time:*** we are lying in the lee of a gravel mound beside the Land Rover, which has been tailing us, with the security vehicles, all day. With his own GPS, Tommy is working out the distance we've covered and studying maps, while Henog, the 'coloured' – as they say here – driver, is helping Adrian cook up a tinned beef casserole. The camels are sitting beside us where I hobbled them, peering into the mist, perhaps wondering if they will get any proper grass instead of lucerne and horse pellets. And where's our farm drinking trough? But these camels must get used to drinking only every two days; eventually, when I'm alone with them, they'll be drinking once a week.

### *6 September*
The early sun shed light like dust around us as I talked to the seated camels, walking about with my tea and bowl of muesli. Mist in eiderdown layers over the mine workings, the metal-roofed complexes that do the job of sorting, washing and resorting the material into a diamond concentrate. But between us and these ghostly buildings, where spotlights ensure it never gets dark, there's the razor-wire fence. One touch of this, according to Tommy, and the security people will be along with their dogs and helicopters.

For the first time I rode Jan. He was soon lagging behind, even though Nelson was busy trying out on Tommy the tricks he once played on me – in particular carrying him off to go and look for water at each windmill. Tommy quickly understood when to cajole and when to fight. However he instinctively rides like a horseman, using his heels, not the reins. He also thinks Nelson is old, but the poor beast only appears to be ancient because he happens to have the settled ways of a country gentleman.

The day bright, the wind flapping us from behind, the south-west, as it will do every day. In our wake beetles wheel away the camel dung, tumbling it to softer sand where they can bury it. A red padloper tortoise stumbles across the road. Two pied crows sit conferring with a smaller species, the black crow. Then the two pied crows leave their gathering, deciding to come along with us.

Now it's twilight, and we are again in the shadow of the Land Rover. I'm now worried about Jan. He's utterly exhausted even though we've done only 25 kilometres, the average I want to achieve in much rougher terrain than this. At feeding time Andries gnawed him on the neck, then budged him away from the lucerne bale. Andries, despite being only three years old, has forced him into third place in the camel hierarchy.

### *7 September*
Woke to find ourselves locked in by mist, the famous Skeleton Coast shroud. Multi-layered, billowing cloud. Nights not too cold if we're in the lee of the vehicle but once you stand up the wind bites, numbing the fingers and slowing the mind.

We managed 35 kilometres, but Jan's still looking strained. I tried to get him to go in front of Nelson, to set his own pace. But he will not: Nelson is Top Camel, and there's nothing we can do. Andries still strolls free at the back, as if on a holiday outing.

THE SKELETON COAST

**Above:** *Cape fur seals* (Arctocephalus pusillus*),
Baker's Bay. In October many more seals join the
colony, the adult males, which can weigh 200
kilos, establishing breeding territories. Staying a
month or two they lose fat as they energetically
mate with their harems (sometimes over fifty
females) and fight off rivals. A year later the pups
are born and the mothers tend their offspring in
hectic nurseries.*

**Left:** *The wreck of* Barge 77 *near Chameis. The
foamy surf is the result of plankton-rich waters,
plankton having been swept north and trapped
along the coast by a sub-oceanic ridge. Though the
whales they supported have almost been hunted
out, the coast still has an extraordinarily high
biomass, fish shoals supporting dolphin (family
Delphinidae), Cape fur seal (Arctocephalus
pusillus*), and fishing birds such as Cape
cormorant (Phalacrocorax capensis*), tern (Sterna
spp.), gull (Larus spp.) and jackass penguin
(Spheniscus demersus*).*

Tommy's skills as a cavalryman show more and more by the day. Now beginning to adjust everything to suit one of his nags – the length of the stirrups, the padding; poor Nelson. Mind you, my own workmanship must be too disorderly for a military man to bear.

Another thing about Tommy: it's often been said that the Germans out here still live in a previous era and his jokes do seem to be of the First World War trenches variety. Tommy: 'Adrian, all your Englander clothes are falling to pieces.'

Adrian: 'See these holey trousers? They're German.'

'Ha! You see? If they had been made by Englanders they would have fallen off already.'

### 8 September

The land begins to buckle and fold. White gravels and black, uncompromising rocks arise from the sands. We have reached Chameis security gate, a checkpoint 112 kilometres from Oranjemund. As we arrived a lorry came through from the Elizabeth Bay diamond mine, near Lüderitz, carrying a huge sealed container full of diamond concentrate. At the gate the guards got out of the escort vehicle and checked the container's padlocks. 'Got any diamonds spare?' I said cheerily to the black driver, hoping he would say something entertaining to my video camera. He looked at me as if I was a highway robber.

'It was only a joke,' I said. The man silently got back into his cab. He drove off; the security escort followed. I said to Tommy, 'Perhaps he doesn't speak English …'

'That remark of yours will go on the computer,' was all Tommy said. It seems I now have a security record.

A short distance away there's a spring burbling out fresh water, and brown hyena tracks criss-cross with those of jackals. Above is an abandoned police outpost from the diamond rush. Entire walls are falling; the old iron beds lie blanketed in sand. Outside you can distinguish ox wagon tracks, preserved in the desert gravels. They lead to a drinking trough big enough to water thirty head of oxen.

But people were here long before the white man and his diamond fever. Above the spring there are limpets lying in neat heaps. Stones lie broken open and notched; there are pieces of ostrich shell fashioned into discs for necklaces. This is a midden, or prehistoric waste heap. Archaeologist Dieter Noli has located 235 prehistoric sites such as these in the Sperrgebiet, some of which are 300,000 years old, and others might prove to be over a million years old. From these people are probably descended those whom we identify as 'Bushmen', nomads who stalked game with their bows and arrows, surviving off water carried in ostrich shells.

Back at the security gate I noticed that Jan was standing well away from the other camels, and kept lifting his front right foot. 'We'd better take a look,' Tommy said. We were both thinking the same: in just this short time the stones had damaged the camels' feet. We found only a small wound, a wet crack in his leathery pad. I have begun treating him with acriflavin in glycerine, yellow stuff like cough mixture. I think we should walk on tomorrow. The inner security zone ends here and we can drop down to the beach, which will be easier on his feet.

### 9 September

To the beach. The camels hadn't been up close to water before – not more than a sheep trough-ful. We led them on foot. It was an important moment, a clue to how they will handle the Lange Wand.

Jan soon forgot about his sore pad. Surf was roaring towards us up the sand, foam boiling off the waves. Nelson wanted nothing to do with all this violence. He allowed us to walk him along the storm beach, but not a step nearer. I decided not to push him too hard, and after a while the camels did start to adjust to the screaming winds and detonating waves. Andries even paused to pick up some mussels to examine. We turned inland from North Rock along a road that has long since been wiped out by sand and repaved with shells.

**Night-time:** this a restless place of high energy. The air moves by violently, slashing you with mists. Waves kick at the shore, tussling with the land.

### 10 September

'I'll go on ahead with the camels,' I said this morning as the others packed up the camp in the wet winds. 'Put some distance down.' But my real reason is just to get away from the rest of the party and their beloved Land Rover. Cooking pots, homely sleeping mattresses. I do understand why it has to keep an eye on us in the Sperrgebiet but I've had three weeks in the dust with the Himba, and three weeks being hammered by camels, and I did that in order to be in communion with the desert, not with the internal combustion engine. Sensing the frustration rising in me, Tommy is letting me go.

My estimation of him continues to increase. He handles me beautifully, like a rogue horse. On occasions like this he steps back, giving me room. He also works hard on Andries. The infant camel simply shrugs off his saddle and runs around, calling to the others to come and join his life of freedom. So much for being a genius – he's more like a delinquent. But again and again Tommy patiently coaxes Andries into the camp, and calms him down, affectionately calling him 'shithead'.

**Left:** *Leading the camels near Baker's Bay. During the second half of the journey I would be alone with them, and out of all contact. It was important to seize any available opportunity to keep developing the camels' trust in me, ready for the time when I would have to ask them to follow me, day after day, into nowhere.*

**Above:** *Black-backed jackals (*Canis mesomelas*) were constant companions near the beach, which they, and brown hyenas (*Hyaena brunnea*), patrolled – the latter for seal pups left unattended by their mothers. During the day jackals often walked nonchalantly alongside the camels; at night, desperate for food, they moved in and even chewed the leather of the saddles.*

There is remarkable gentleness within the big man.

As I walked away, triumphant to be allowed into the Sperrgebiet with only the camels, a jackal came our way up the track. It didn't pause but just veered to the side to avoid getting trampled on. This is an important reminder: the jackal has little knowledge of humans – no one else has had the privilege of travelling by foot through the Sperrgebiet since its formation, and I mustn't moan.

Alone with the diamond sands … I couldn't help but let my eyes stray to the ground. The trick I'm told is to look for sharp angles – diamonds, being so hard, are often like splinters. Unfortunately, it's a prison sentence even for picking up a diamond here.

For years, traders, soldiers and explorers had tramped through this place while the diamonds were just lying there twinkling, the wind sorting and resorting them. In 1865 one syndicate, the Pomona Mining Company, was actually shovelling through sands which were to produce the most dramatic diamond rush of all. Alas, they were looking for silver and lead. August Stauch, the German who was to make that first discovery, came out on a two-year contract with the railways, hoping a spell in the dry climate would be good for his asthma. The ship docked in May 1907 at the desolate port of Lüderitzbucht. There is little in Lüderitz nowadays, but then there was a lot less – just a few corrugated buildings, the surrounding desert, and sometimes, when the battering wind dropped, a cold fog. Fresh water was scarce, supplemented by ship from Cape Town.

Stauch was told he would be a supervisor at Grasplatz, the first siding out of Lüderitz. He had the job of keeping the line free from the ever-hungry elements. A man of diverse interests, he asked his labourers to bring him any interesting stones they found. It was in April 1908, while shovelling the railway embankment sand, that a coloured labourer, Zacharias Lewala, spotted something shiny. He peered closer. It was a crystal. He handed it to the foreman. 'Meneer, *n' mooi klip.* Sir, a pretty stone,' he said – or so the legend goes. The foreman passed it on to Stauch, who scratched it against the glass face of his watch. It left a groove. Very soon after that, the railwayman was to be found pacing around armed with claim stakes. Methodically and discreetly, he began pegging out the sand. Before anyone had realized what he was up to he had resigned from his job, got financial backing from his former railway bosses and begun establishing claims everywhere.

He had almost two months' start before his diamonds were officially identified in Swakopmund and the stampede began in earnest. Sailors deserted ships, guano diggers their bird droppings, the town baker his loaves. Ox wagons, mules and camels launched out into the wastes, bearing their hopeful masters. Down the men got on their stomachs, and began searching the ground. Sun glared off sands rich in mica [glittering silicate scales], the winds blasted, fogs numbed. Labourers were brought in to search on their bellies too – they wore a pouch around their neck to put the diamonds into, and gags over their mouths to stop them swallowing them. The government joined the rush, official parties setting out secretly at night to claim, at random, as much of each valley as they could. By 1913–14, 1,570,000 carats were being extracted within the Sperrgebiet, the new exclusion zone to which Stauch and other existing miners were given rights. For all the might and machinery of Namdeb (then known as CDM) it was a figure they didn't match until 1967, when they'd been in existence forty-eight years.

No such luck for me, Nelson, Jan and Andries. I turned towards the sea again. In the distance the thunder of waves, water relentlessly grinding the rocks, and the wind knocking the tops off waves. Easy to see why the coast was almost ignored for two hundred years after the fifteenth-century Portuguese navigators first put ashore as they felt their way around the Cape, looking for a route through to the East. This was Baker's Bay, high rollers thumping on to long beaches, smashing on crags. Cape gannets in the wind, and Cape fur seals swirling in the white water. In the distance, trying to make use of what little cover there was, a strandwolf or brown hyena, its long black lion's mane parted by the wind. It was patrolling the beach, seeking out seal pups to snatch. Striped legs, huge front paws, its large shoulders are strong enough even to drag an adult seal, its jaws to crunch a skull.

I was so busy watching the seals, the waves, the cunning strandwolf – so much movement after the steady fixed landscape of the Kalahari – that I was startled to look down at my feet and find that our path was blocked by a pool left by the high tide. Nelson decided he wasn't going to take a step further. The other camels drew up behind, using him as a shield. It was Andries who broke the spell. Curious at the light coming off the water, he came round from the back and dabbed at it with his front feet. Nelson copied. Soon all three camels were poking their feet into the water like English bathers braving chilly surf. Then they walked on, stamping their feet exuberantly in the pool, enjoying the cool water as it trickled down their tummies.

Beyond the bay, the coast road sunk down among the rock ledges. Sand from the beach spun overhead, settling inland in whatever hollows gave it shelter. The road itself was again lost to embryo dunes here, and when I turned around I found our tracks in the sand were already gone. An uncomfortable sensation. We were insignificant. Our mark on the world was being wiped out.

Here the road seemed to have given up years ago, and I was forced down on to the beach. It was a noisy, terrible place – it was so bad I even wished for a sight of the Land Rover. Nelson wasn't at all happy with the surf crashing in, but I found that by positioning him on the left, the side he likes best, with Andries in the middle and Jan tucked in on the right – out of kicking range – we could make progress. Nelson walked stoically along, eyeing the spitting surf, the creamy throth that flashed over the sand towards his flat feet.

Now it's late evening, and I'm united with Tommy and the gang – I'm writing while they sleep. We've arrived at Dreimasterpunt, an old German station – though you'd hardly know it. One of the few signs that people have ever been here is a narrow-gauge railway, the rails now in needle splinters. I've come to realize that Henog is rather interesting. He sports a gold ring in his ear, yet turns out to be an ex-policeman. He's devoted to his wife, whom he calls Kleintjie, 'Little One', yet has had five children, all by different contented women.

I think about these things as I lie awake, looking at the stars. A strandwolf hovers about with some young jackals, waiting for a chance to sneak in and grab anything. It's true that my lips are beginning to blister – brushing my teeth is now painful – and I have sores developing on my unwashed, camel-soiled skin, but this desert seems to be strengthening me, not weakening me as I feared. Perhaps later I will not have to fear sad thoughts of home.

### 11 September, some 20 kilometres north of Bogenfels

A family of jackals walked with me, through green rock-chip hills. When I stopped, they stopped. They sat quickly, in a flash hidden in the brown dust. It was eerie being watched. The camels became agitated.

It's dark now. We are camped in a valley of white quartz shingle and sliced honey rock, with salt-bush clusters. We've walked 36 kilometres through mist, white sunshine, and now hurtling wind – a killer if you face it. Even riding in the same direction the afternoon winds have been doing me damage, irritating abscesses – possibly from spider bites – that are fast developing on my neck and right hand.

I'm watching Tommy, this man whose eyes are sometimes very alive, sometimes dull with scorn. I need to know how he works, how easily he rises to temper. Tommy must also be judging me. I know we'll be up against it together after Lüderitz, entering the Namib-Naukluft Park. My biggest worry is that his military background has taught him self-discipline, but for all his blusterings it's not natural for him. I can expect mistakes to slip through.

For now we converse easily, usually about the camels – the state of Jan's foot (which is much better) and the state of Andries (who is becoming a problem child). Nelson, we both agree, has one serious flaw – a dread of soft sand. The

*Towards Elizabeth Bay Mine, passing a whale skeleton. Once the bleak coast seemed to offer nothing but misery, whaling and the lucrative guano deposits of its shore birds. However, a tributary of the Orange River, the Modder, ran through the Kimberley diamond fields of South Africa and in 1890 Cecil Rhodes helped organize an expedition into present-day Namibia, suspecting that diamonds might also have been washed downriver to the coast. Unfortunately, prospecting was halted by the Germans, who for another eighteen years remained ignorant of the fortune scattered there.*

dunes come in three sorts here in the Namib – linear dunes, with the sand piled up in long lines, so-called 'streets', in between; stellar dunes, arranged into star shapes by cross winds, and the dunes we'll come to tomorrow, the barchan (also known as crescent or wandering) dunes. Trouble is, as Tommy has pointed out, Nelson actually observes his surroundings.

### 12 September, 46 kilometres clocked up, nearing Lüderitz

Woke to find that the saddles have been chewed by jackals during the night. Poor, famished creatures. We rode off through biscuit crags, formations like burnt loaves. The hills are smooth, and the valleys between often heaped with ditched sand. Some ditched by the wind, some by man. For we were now entering

Pomona, cause of the greatest excitement in the early years.

August Stauch reasoned that, as the perennial winds and currents were from the south, this must be the origin of the diamonds. He bundled together more stakes and headed out from Lüderitz into the desert. This time he was accompanied by Professor Robert Scheibe, a distinguished geologist, and equipped with mules and wagons. After a fruitless day Stauch was riding his horse back to camp when he came across a Herero labourer, Jakob, gathering firewood. He told him to forget the wood and look for diamonds. He'd meant it as a joke, but Jakob dropped to the ground and next thing, he began calling out: 'Mister! *Ai je titatita*!' He cupped his hand and began filling it with diamonds. Both Jakob's hands were soon full and he was having to store the diamonds in his mouth. '*Ein Märchen*!' A fairytale! was Scheibe's response when he was told, and the place became known as Fairytale Valley. As the moon rose, Stauch and Scheibe went outside and gazed down the valley. The diamonds were shining like stars in the night.

Since then a whole town's population has been and gone, each valley's content been shovelled and sieved. The houses are still standing, but are now only sand traps. Telephone wires twitch in the wind, sand hurtles through broken windows, dropping into stairways, halls, living rooms. Bricks, corrugated iron, everything is being reduced by the elements, forcibly made to rejoin them. Dust to dust … In front of a proud little house are the remains of flower beds, still kerbed in white stone. The yellow blossom of a single aloe tree is more poignant than anything. It alone succeeds in maintaining its dignity. All else has surrendered – the town graveyard looks no sadder than the high street. This was once a place of triumph – well over a million carats in the first two years. Large scale mining ceased here in 1931 with the Great Depression. The town now counts for nothing.

The camels didn't like the place – the sudden bangs of window frames, the streets now leading nowhere. Pressed on, worrying even more about Jan, who is getting slower and slower. The wind blew up, buffeting us. Sand lifted and flew, streaming into our faces even as we sat up on the camels. It began to hurt, reddening our eyes, further irritating the sores on my neck and hand – they need a doctor's attention now. We wound through our first dunes. These were the anticipated barchans, formed into a crescent with the ends facing forward.

As it happened, the camels were again not put fully to the test. There were spaces between these sickle-shaped sand heaps, and we were able to side-step all the serious slopes. But I saw enough to know that we were right – approaching dunes Nelson holds back, swerves – anything rather than face a slope. Unexpectedly, Jan proves to be sure-footed.

We shall be sleeping in the lee of a crescent dune, its steep face encompassing us, bothering us with gusting eddies. Sand everywhere, most noticeable in our ears, mouth and nose. When the wind surges, the sand stings hard, and rasps. The camels sit chewing the cud regardless, just closing their nostril slits and batting their long eyelashes.

### 13 September

*Morning:* my neck and hand sores have now become the sort of scarlet mounds that are scary to look at. But today, on schedule, we'll reach Lüderitz.

Down through the mists we can see Elizabeth Bay. The mine, built only in 1991, stands ghostly in the haze – pipes, towers, giant lorries and conveyor belts. It's all a long way from Stauch's shovel and jig.

*Later:* as we went by, mammoth dumper trucks shook the ground, conveyor belts trundled. It was as if we had entered a giant child's sandpit. We wound our way next through dry stony hills scattered with Bushman's candle, a low succulent whose inflammable, waxy stem saves it from desiccation. At last, through another arid pass, we were met by a roll of barbed wire and a security patrol – the end of the Sperrgebiet. We dismounted and were searched. The camels got the treatment too. Nelson bellowed, his eyes following the nervous guard's hands as he frisked the 450-kilogram beast. First he fingered the saddle and around his hump and then he investigated, hesitantly, behind Nelson's ears. Didn't go down well.

We trotted up a windy road to Lüderitz and Gary's stables, an outlying spot by a lagoon. The angular, austere German houses were visible on the hills. Not knowing quite what was required for camels, Gary had made a gigantic kraal that even three mammoths would have loved. The camels saw it, and accelerated. There was nothing that Tommy and I could do to slow them down – they'd seen a home. Then the camels saw Gary's two precious horses cantering forward, offering a challenge. The horses caught the camel smell, and stood stock still. No wonder Gary regarded them as special – from the stories I've heard, most horses run for miles at that first wild whiff of camel. But these two stood panting at us, defiantly swinging their heads before finally trotting aside. Nelson marched on. Andries trotted behind, carefree as ever. Jan collapsed in a sad heap to let me off – unable, it seemed, to get me five paces further, to the kraal itself.

# 5

# THE LONG WALL

**14 September, Lüderitz**

I've just returned from feeding the camels in the kraal. They sit all day, calmly waiting for the next snack from their new admirers.

Gone are the frenetic diamond-rush days when there were horse races in the desert and a choice of seven brothels. Now this is a quiet town with a dustless main street. Cars and a sprinkling of people meander slowly down it. Every day seems to be Sunday. Yet even after a day in Lüderitz I feel cramped. I'm longing for the desert again. It seems illogical. What did it give us but howling winds, painful sand blasts and blistered lips? The answer is that it gave us space, and we expanded to fill it. The town is now too small. It's also a disruption – it threatens to soften my determination to face the winds again. As it is, I'm weakened by my abscesses, which have given me a slight fever. Dr Marais has put me on antibiotics, and told me to delay my departure because of the angry red one on my finger. 'If it turns nasty out in the desert' – he points out of his surgery window – 'you'll lose it.'

In the street no one stares at my sores, my coat of dust. I look like just one more young man who's been scratching optimistically in the desert for a missed diamond. However, the word is out that the 'camelman' (as the newspapers call me) has arrived. Hateful stares from one old woman – a dog lover who's heard

*The Lange Wand , where towering dunes meet the sea. Never having seen much more than a bucket of water before their arrival at the Orange River, the camels were now up against the South Atlantic.*

of that *Times* article, 'Behave camels – or this man will have you …'. Others, who feel they should have been allowed to make this journey before me, snarl behind my back – I'm cruel with the camels, arrogant in my reluctance to use vehicles. 'The conservation men use 4 x 4s – why isn't that good enough for him?' In Namibia, there's a scepticism about outsiders, a possessiveness of what they have – which, after all, is – I can tell already – a very special desert.

At lunchtime in a bar with the latest generation of prospectors, I did find – once you've proved that you aren't a threat – a generosity to strangers. After all, they were strangers here themselves a year, a month ago. So I sat down with one group and talked about the journey. Like the diamonds themselves, these men have a lustre and hardness. They've been sorted by their dreams from ordinary society, filtered from South Africa, Britain, Ireland, Zimbabwe. Over a beer they loosened up, wished me luck, slapped me on the back: 'Fellow pioneers.'

Lüderitz was once a man's town. It still is. The sands may have been virtually sieved clean of diamonds, but the seas haven't. Diamond divers work the concessions in the surf zone, plunging from boats into the turbulent water, wielding vacuum pumps. Small contractor operations just like these declared 132,529 carats last year, or 10 per cent of total Namdeb production. At the moment they've been landlocked for three weeks because of the high winds. Bad enough for a sailor anywhere in the world to feel the breeze and not put to sea, but in Lüderitz it's a prison sentence. They are trapped between violent seas and violent sands – the forbidden Sperrgebiet to the south, the closed Namib-Naukluft Park to the north. Their frustrations, stoked by dreams, are fired up. The word is that Stefan, owner of the Restaurant at the End of the Universe, has a birthday some time around now. Unknown to him, everyone will be piling in there to celebrate it tonight.

## 15 September

Usually when the divers assemble at his restaurant Stefan has to take down all the pictures. Last night, it had to be done for him. Soon champagne was spraying the ceiling, beer emptying over heads. There were ice-cube battles, lipstick graffiti drawn over the staggering Stefan's forehead, men hugging.

After dispatching a fax to the BBC asking them to send an indignant letter to *The Times*, walked down to see the camels. Gary was there to help us hold down Jan while we inspected his foot. He's a diamond diver, a free spirit like his beloved horses. Plaits his long hair just like their tails. Tommy turned up with a 'camel shoe' he's been crafting from leather for Jan's sore foot. Hopeless – off in a second. And when Tommy turned his back on Jan, he tried to get him with those surprisingly quick knees of his. Tommy also surprisingly quick on his feet.

Gradually, we are gearing up for the final section in which I'll be accompanied by Tommy: through the Namib-Naukluft Park to Walvis Bay. I'm getting more and more moral support from the citizens of Lüderitz – my journey makes many white people think back nostalgically to tales of the German Camel Corps which helped open up this country, and today a schoolmistress gave me a spare white tablecloth with tassels which will serve as a scarf against the sand and sun. All this is helped by Tommy and his wife Marion, both of whom have backed me to the hilt. Based here, Tommy is held in high esteem – admired and sometimes loathed for his incorruptibility. He stalks poachers like a wild cat. No one, not even his brother who runs a butchery in Swakopmund, is allowed a second chance if caught with a dead ostrich in his fridge. Nor are children spared from this battle. Hoping to outmanoeuvre him, the poachers get their offspring to ask Rodney and Andrew at school where their father is. 'I've had to teach my own children to lie,' Tommy said. And I know this hurts him deep inside.

### 16 September

The camels restless – like the diamond divers, needing to rid themselves of energy. They are now intolerant of foolish humans who lean on the kraal and fawn over them. Jan especially irritable, blowing air from puffed cheeks. 'Paa-paa-paa-paa!' We keep meaning to put up a notice saying: 'Dangerous Animals.'

But Gary's horses certainly don't think of them as a threat. They trot about trying to oust the camels from their home. We found one actually inside the camel kraal, startling our beasts with its speed. Nelson and Jan horrified, Andries badly frightened.

Final preparations for arrival in Walvis Bay, the other side of the Namib-Naukluft Park, where the camels will be housed at the riding stables. Mrs Kleyenstüber, who runs a flower shop, has advised the committee that my scheming camels are on their way. All the young girls practising for forthcoming gymkhanas are being advised to get their training in while they can.

My last pitched battle against the Land Rover, which the government is determined shall accompany me. Tommy has again talked through the dangers out there and I do see their point – though I'd still give it a go. What do I value in the desert other than emptiness, a blank page not written on by the West? And what is a vehicle other than a capsule of the Western world?

But no one else seems to agree – and I know, as Adrian says, that I'm being unrealistic. This journey is not going to happen without someone coming with me – in the south of the park there are additional legal restrictions due to the presence of diamonds, and of course I have already used vehicles elsewhere to set the expedition up. Besides, Tommy is a family man and can't be expected to take much more of a risk. He's risking his career as it is, by agreeing to limit us to just one vehicle. Geologists from Elizabeth Bay Mine gave a unanimous gasp at what he's planning to do.

Already Tommy has sat me down in his office, rolled out the maps, reminded me what happened to the early pioneers. Some got through – most famously, Dr E. Reuning's expedition from Lüderitz to Swakopmund in 1912. But others lost camels on the way, and some didn't make it at all. But in all cases, conditions were easier – there were open springs, Hottentot guides. And during the diamond rush there were whole populations of labourers out there. The unpopular Sperrgebiet, though recognizing the prior claims of those like Stauch, forced new prospectors north up the coast. Up to 3000 Ovambos worked on the northern field between Conception Bay and Meob Bay. Now these places are once more desert, the jigs, bottles and boots of the prospectors all but buried. In the 1960s and 1970s expeditions (documented by Dr Hellwig) did trace all the old spring sites, but it was an arduous business even for those heavily equipped teams. For us there'll be nothing but our two depots, one at the Bulldozer, a site named after a vehicle abandoned out there, and one at Fischersbrunn, the only spring not blown over by sand.

As a special concession to me, Adrian is being given permission to join Henog in the Land Rover – partly because Adrian happens to be a trained mechanic. But other problems are emerging. Extremely high seas have washed away the sand behind Black Rock, the high point where we were hoping to rest midway along the Lange Wand. And other passages along the beach are now very soft – Nelson's pet hate. So we'll have to take an inland route along a dune street and drop down to the sea halfway along the Lange Wand.

*Later:* another problem. Tommy has already organized a water depot at the Bulldozer, but the one at the diamond outpost of Fischersbrunn has not been set up yet. The conservation officer Achim Lenssen, who has generously agreed to drop bales of lucerne for the camels there, has been temporarily blinded by a spitting cobra. He was at his washbasin when he noticed a movement down the plughole. He bent over just in time to see a darting tongue. The snake spat. Excruciating pain. His wife doused his eyes with milk to soothe them, then sped him to hospital. He'll be all right, but the cornea has to regrow in one eye. Achim will drop my supplies at Fischersbrunn later, and, as the foremost authority of the northern Namib-Naukluft Park and a formidable navigator, he is rather expecting me to want to rendezvous with him there.

*With Tommy Hall, while hobbling Jan in front of the diamond-mine manager's*
*house in the ghost town of Kolmanskop. An ex-horse-cavalry man who fought against*
*SWAPO 'freedom fighters', Tommy works as a conservation officer for his former adversaries,*
*now in government – this spirit of co-operation typical of the new country. Fluent in the*
*Damara language, which he learnt as a child playing with Damara children, he*
*is universally respected in his fight against poachers.*

### 17 September

The day before departure. I came into Tommy's office to begin final packing. Henog and Adrian already loading the Land Rover – presumably assembling sand ladders, shovels, all the things needed to keep the machine out of trouble. Tommy announced, standing behind his desk, 'Something important: Jan almost killed a woman yesterday.'

I grabbed my video camera to record a rather promising-sounding story. It seems that one of Tommy's sons saw the whole thing. He warned the woman not to go into the kraal. She told the boy to mind his own business and went right on in, proffering a bunch of grass. She handed it to Jan – Jan, of all camels … He was suspicious of the woman, and slow accepting the gift. She snatched it away, impatiently. It was enough to set him off. He did his special double knee-kick, smoothly knocking her flat, with a view to sitting on her. At that stage the wretched woman's poor husband appeared, and dragged her to safety. Who she is, we don't know. She was white and middle-aged. A black man, an Ovambo, tried the same thing later. He got the same treatment. Strange to think I'm friends with such a lethal animal.

Later I went down to the kraal myself. I met Dr Marais, who was having a look at the famous camels. Got him to do an instant update on my sores. He's pleased with the abscess on my neck – a huge Martian crater. The other needs 'minor surgery.'

I walked up to Jan to give him a final check. He began puffing his cheeks angrily, hanging threateningly over me. Told him not to be silly and to sit down, which he did. He was still very tense. As I patted his cheek, he snapped at me. But his foot has healed and by the end of the examination he had calmed down. I judged him fit – his feet have to negotiate only three days of hard gravel before the sands begin. We'll leave tomorrow as planned. We are all growing too comfortable here.

Will we make it? I think so, though Tommy's mind is not properly focused. It's not his fault. According to his spies, the poachers are watching, waiting for him to leave with me. They will go for gemsbok and ostrich. What they don't know is that Tommy has secretly negotiated with Namdeb, who will extend their sophisticated diamond security operation to run extra patrols during his absence.

**_18 September_**

The big 'off'. Adrian tinkering with cameras – his Nikons are already in ruins, and we are on number four out of the five video cameras. I went to the doctor and came away rather pleased with myself, having filmed the operation with one hand while the other was being sliced open. Dr Marais said, afterwards, 'In two days you have to make a decison – whether to turn back to have it treated.' He said he understands the pressure we are under.

I donned my new scarf, the tablecloth with tassels. Final goodbyes from the crowd, which seemed more interested in the camels' fate than ours – especially that of the lovable Andries, who ambled dreamily behind us, and soon (luckily out of sight) neatly slipped off his saddle and load.

We took the ride slowly – the camels were stiff. Rode out along the railway line towards Kolmanskop, near where August Stauch found that first diamond. A rock kestrel launched from a crag. A black-breasted snake eagle wound through the turbulence. I watched it climb – the only eagle which will feed in mid-air. It swallows its prey, and if it doesn't feel comfortable regurgitates and swallows again. It kills snakes by snapping their spines, or dropping them from a very great height.

Most of the residential houses of Kolmanskop are still standing, but there are none of the magnificent lawns, roses, and eucalyptus trees that were once nurtured here with the help of expensively imported water. Before the settlement was abandoned in 1956, there had been a butcher, a baker and an ice-plant which distributed ice to each household door. In 1917 a social hall was built, complete with gymnasium and skittle alley. I dismounted Jan and went to have a look around the manager's house. All walls upright, but divided by cracks as if from an earthquake. A wide staircase led up invitingly to a roof with gaping wide holes. Flowery wallpaper that had been chosen, cherished, abandoned with everything else. Windows affording views of rolling desert. I think I expected ghost towns to be spooky. In fact the opposite is true. These human reminders are comforting; it's good to know that the deserts were once a home to intruders like yourself.

### 19 September

Closer attention has to be paid to navigation now – as we ride, I consult my compass. Tommy favours his hand held GPS, data beaming down to him from half a dozen satellites, telling him where he is, where he's going.

The horizon is lifting itself up – the first hint of the great dunes ahead. The crescent dunes to our left and right are small, but are like sand muscles, flexing. The only animals near at hand are the beetles trundling fast by. And once I saw a pink, lacy sand snake. Nelson didn't, and trod square on it. I felt sorry for the snake as it squirmed there, squashed by the only camel for a hundred years.

We are camped in a hollow, Tommy studying the maps, Adrian steaming up the Land Rover with his cooking. Around us are cream gravel plains, sooty hills far off. We did 11 kilometres yesterday, 38 today through sharp gravels. All the camels' feet have suffered noticeably since Lüderitz. The pads are wearing away, layer after layer. The sooner we are into the dunes, tomorrow, the better.

Tommy has just heard on his radio that the poachers have made their move, as predicted. Details sketchy, but Namdeb's security men chased some vehicles through the dunes and arrested dozens. While on the subject of security, I asked to have a look at Tommy's Czech pistol. He gave me a demonstration, shocking me by managing to shoot a barely visible bush 50 metres away. 'This is an unusual handgun,' he said, putting it back in its holster as if the pistol had done all the work.

### 20 September

Achieved 34 kilometres through soft pebble sands, followed all day by two pied crows which stopped when we stopped and sat making rude gurgling noises. I

**Right:** *The linear dunes of the Namib-Naukluft, with streets between providing clear passageways running to the north-west for 150 kilometres.*

**Above:** *The nara melon* (Acanthosicyos horridus). *Although apparently thriving in waterless sands, the nara extends long roots to subterranean waters and is not really a true desert plant. The plant is dioecious, having separate females and males, and also has photosynthesizing stems and thorns, rather than leaves, to discourage grazers and to protect its fruit from all but a handful of mammals, such as the porcupine* (Hystrix africaeaustralis).

like to think they are the same two crows that we picked up at Oranjemund, the same ones that uttered gurgling noises behind us throughout the Sperrgebiet.

At first, to our right and left were dry, burnt-biscuit hills. Maroon dust, the dense garnet that often settles down with diamonds, was scattered lightly in hollows. The black hills were dusted with yellow sand, blown into impossibly high valley traps. Ahead, a huge white band, the start of the dunes. 'That's nothing,' Tommy said.

The first true dunes came soon afterwards. They began with a small ridge, a wiggling crest. 'A baby,' Tommy said. Then they grew. 'The mothers,' Tommy said. Red, inactive-looking, the sands ahead were in parallel lines – the streets, one of which would deliver us safely north-west through the sand fields. Nelson began grumbling. He stopped to look, incredulously, into the void. All the camels were slowing down, giving us time to change our minds.

Now we are camped on the ridge, a gentle old dune crest. The only sound is the rapid clacking smack of the barking geckos. This is the far end of the Koichab Valley, the very brink of the dunes – the point of no return. We pick a dune street, and head down it. But before we leave tomorrow, we'll check to see what my finger is like.

### 21 September

My finger is less angry, Jan's foot is fine. We've decided to commit. On then, taking the fourth street along from the west.

'Street' conjures visions of traffic, but the greatest impression these give is one of emptiness. The street is 2 kilometres wide here, and contains only one obvious plant species, the nara. However, there must be other life – after all, the nara has tough photosynthesizing stems, rather than leaves, to avoid being eaten up. And in the first, still moments of the day we could indeed see traces of night activity – those of golden moles, as they'd swum through the sand shallows, and the parallel whip marks of a sidewinder adder. As we rode on, the list lengthened. Bat-eared fox, Cape fox, black-backed jackal, Cape hare, gerbil, legless lizard. The prickly melons of the female nara plants had clearly been bitten open by porcupines and hyenas – the pips inside have an almond taste, and the Topnaar Hottentots of the Namib's Kuiseb Valley make them into cakes.

***Midday:*** Andries has just thrown off his saddle again – wiggled his bottom and was suddenly free. Tommy used his cavalry skills to bring him in. At these times, Tommy becomes acutely sensitive – a listener instead of a commander. He will surprise us all by softening, and opening himself up. I'm tempted to say it's a battle between his German and English halves. He will calmly reassure Andries –

'Ah, Shithead …' – and gently wipe his underarm odour on Andries' nose – a horseman's trick to get the animal used to his smell. However, on this occasion Andries suddenly broke away from him again, thumping the Land Rover with his foot and breaking off a tail light. Childish of me, but I can't help getting a little pleasure from the slow demise of the vehicle – intruder, traitor, imperialist. Its bits keep falling off and increasingly it's getting stuck in the sand.

That's not to say the camels progress effortlessly. Jan still not on top of things. Each morning, we wake to find strands of lucerne hanging from his fur, and throth from where another camel – suspicion points to Andries – has nibbled at him.

## 22 September

Went for a walk at dawn to try to catch the last of the desert's nightlife. All around me signs of where the golden mole had gone into action, now that the sands had cooled, paddling along the surface to snap up crickets and beetles. The palmato gecko was pattering about – it's equipped with web feet to give it an edge on the insects it pursues through loose sand. All these animals chasing not just food but also water through the desert, passing this vital commodity around – from the beetle which drinks from the fog, and is eaten by the mole, which sustains a fox, whose faeces nurtures a dung beetle, and on and on.

Advancing up the dune street, the sides darkly clouded with magnetite; 34 kilometres done. Jan, I feel, is slowing – too early to tell for sure. Andries revels in the freedom this desert gives him – once he has dumped his saddle.

We saw only six species of life in the whole day – ourselves, the camels, the nara melon plant, the spiky desert grass, three identical black tenebrionid beetles, and a sidewinder adder. The camels were, as usual, oblivious to the snake. It spiralled over the sand and in the shade of a grass clump formed a tight circle where it flexed and writhed, submerging itself. Soon it was all hidden except the diamond head with its multicoloured scales, each like a grain of sand. The snake peered out, waiting in the cool sand to strike at lizards or beetles. It will drink at dawn, licking condensation from its skin.

Apparently one of the Land Rover's 'coil springs' has gone. It's too much to hope that they will abandon the vehicle. Foolishly, I said so, and Tommy overheard.

'You'd be the first to die out here.' Anger in his voice. I deserved it.

**Overleaf:** *Spencer Bay, and the 1945 wreck of the steamer,* Otavi, *seen through the legendary mists of the Skeleton Coast.*

'I know,' I said, appeasing him. But I've already worked it out, and actually I'll be the last. First to die will be Adrian. Not his fault – he wasn't expecting to be allowed out here, and simply isn't prepared or fit. Next Tommy: unfit, but his bullheadedness and army discipline will pull him a long way. Then Henog, a tough character whose killer instinct will ensure his own survival. Finally Benedict: I'm very fit and strong in my mind – some of this due to baking with the Himba. And even if I hadn't been, on countless previous mis-adventures I've proved surprisingly indestructible for someone so skinny and slightly vague.

We made a trip out to the Bulldozer, a vehicle abandoned in the late 1940s. Once it was a glorious earth-mover, now it's a victim of the moving earth. The engine seized, and all it does now is serve as a reference point for passing aircraft. We only want to use it as a water dump – our last until we're the other side of the fearful Lange Wand. We let Nelson drink his fill and he gulped down 75 litres.

### 23 September

Trying, with some difficulty, to enter into the spirit of things by acknowledging that there is some purpose to the Land Rover. We left the camels behind and took it on a reconnaissance trip through to the coast at Spencer Bay, about 35 kilometres away WSW. There was no route known to humanity through the dunes at 5.30 a.m., when we set off, and there still isn't one. We gave up at midday, still 16 kilometres away. A freak rain shower shot at us, the wind gathered, swung and whipped us. Sand spun out from the ridges in long yellow smoky tongues. Wisps of it snaked over flats, wrapping around our legs. The Land Rover was caught time and time again atop dune crests. We crawled underneath, digging the help-less machine free. Coming away, Tommy's face was masked by sand like a mole's. Adrian's Nikon lenses were sand-blasted and he used his camera-cleaning brush to empty out his ears.

Back at the camp now: an elephant shrew has just bounced over my foot, waving its trunk. Perhaps more indicative of the desert's capricious nature, an electric storm blew up from nowhere. It created a fuggy stillness – during which we hurriedly erected tents for the first time – and then blew in. My tent bounced away into the night, rolling off like tumbleweed. Haven't seen it since.

The state of Jan is a continuing worry. He is always tired. And at mealtimes Andries has taken to pecking at him – Jan is the underdog again. But he still has an appetite – last night while everyone else was sleeping I watched him lift Henog's shoes and put them gently down again. He is desperate for me to give him something other than horse pellets.

### 24 September, 28 kilometres from last night's camp

Reached another symbol of man's folly, the Lorry. Bought cheap after the war, the Ford wears camouflage paint and crayoned on it is a lot number from an auction. Its trailer carries a huge toolbox and dozens of sardine cans, now rusted away. The fish lie desiccated, like fossils. In the Namib, all elements combine to undo man – the heat, wind, earth, even the angry mists of the coast.

Andries, after a day spent romping at a safe distance from us, evading all attempts at capture, finally walked into the camp wondering where his food was. Tommy led him smartly off for a training session. 'You are a shithead. What are you? Shithead. But we are going to get on fine, ja?'

### 25 September

Tommy announced we would be staying in camp – waiting, would you believe it, for a breakdown vehicle. It will be guided here – with difficulty, presumably – by Dieter Noli, the desert archaeologist. Struggling very hard to be reasonable about this, I took the camels away from the camp, stalked by Adrian and his cameras. These moments spent alone leading the camels may prove crucial. Once we get to Walvis Bay I'll be by myself. Will they follow me when they know there's no one around to bring reinforcements?

Besides, I'm happier with just the squeaking of the saddles, the padding of flat feet on sand. Adrian and I had a short picnic by a granite mound which pokes from the sands near here. Smoothed by the wind, it shines a leaden grey light, the parallel ridges on it like those of a fallen dragon's ribcage.

Back at the camp, the repair people were finishing up. They chucked their beer cans into the back of the Lorry, then took it in turns to ride like Hell's Angels through the sands, spinning about like juveniles. 'They're excited,' Tommy said, apologetically. 'No one gets the chance to be out here.'

But it was depressing seeing the desert used as a plaything, the beginning of the loss of perhaps its greatest worth to the world: a place in which the crammed human species can stand back and take a look at itself.

### 26 September

On, on, on. The Land Rover is often hopelessly behind.

Tommy now riding Nelson exactly as if he were a horse. He gees him up, clucks with his mouth the way horsey people do. We've done 47 kilometres (27 a day on average, even with a rest day). The dune street has petered out, as expected. We are now working across to the Lange Wand, struggling to find our way north-west through sand lying in disarray.

**Left:** *In the Namib-Naukluft. Contrary to popular belief, camels fare badly in dunes, their hump and long legs giving them a high centre of gravity. Though I'd painstakingly trained the camels to overcome their instinctive fear of slopes, it was only now that they were put to the test. Nelson (foreground) would often gaze ahead to see what lay in wait on the horizon – a behavioural characteristic of camels which helps them avoid expending valuable energy in the desert.*

**Above:** *The incoming tide licking the base of the Lange Wand dunes, cutting us off.*

Inevitably, tension rising between all of us. Henog swanks around, annoying Adrian. I am silently angry with the Land Rover, which is preventing us from exposing ourselves to the desert. Tommy is openly frustrated with me for not joyfully joining in camp activities: 'Benedict is being a shit today.' He longs for fresh water to splash in at Fischersbrunn, the isolated mining outpost. It's uninhabited, but perhaps the only building out here without a sand-drift inside it.

For today, we have managed to avoid the steepest of the dunes. We steered the camels through them on foot, our group like a little vessel caught in huge seas. Around us the slopes rose and fell, waves on a caramel sea caught in time. We are camped now among these waves – the sand ocean around us is silent, vast, spacious. People from around the world who've given up the nomadic lifestyle – Westerners, Easterners, but in our precious civilizations all of us cluttered, buffered from the elements – have always been drawn to the desert by just these qualities. And now by an additional reason: the desert is fairly undisturbed. We haven't quite mucked up this bit of the planet yet.

## 27 September

Cutting through to the sea. Before we set out, I sat on a dune with a fog-basking beetle. On early mornings such as these it sets itself up on the top of the slipface, pointing into the wind, lowering its head and lifting its back. The mist condenses on the raised shield, and water dribbles down to collect around its mouthparts.

I could have stayed watching it drink, but it was time to face the dunes. This would be the first big test. I gathered the three camel reins in my hand and led the animals on foot. Adrian behind somewhere with his Nikons and Henog was also on foot, guiding Tommy (in the Land Rover) through these complex dune fields.

The camels progressed tentatively, feeling with their front pads, Nelson instantly coming to a halt whenever the sands softened. They played for time, standing urinating, thinking about the awful slope awaiting them. It was painstaking. All other desert animals moved quicker than us. The Namib sand-diver, or shovel-nosed lizard, would, at a blink, plunge for safety. And then there was *Onymacris plana*, my favourite tenebrionid beetle, with a wizened shell like a flat black nut: the fastest beetle in the world, it dashed about on slipfaces, hoping to catch the odd seed or tasty dead fly.

The sea breeze hit us suddenly: the air cooling, not scorching. And when we did see the sea itself – it lay beyond twenty more waves of sand – we could discern a humpback whale cruising by, sieving the plankton-rich currents, its spout shooting from blue waters.

Today was a fine day – we were meant to be feeling lucky. It was hardly possible, standing on the dune ridge in the buffeting wind, to imagine the place in normal weather – the driving mist, the shrieking cold. Yet not far down the coast at Sylvia Hill – near Naribis, the place where there's fresh water in the tidal sands – are circles of quartz, the bases of huts fashioned from skins. Two skeletons found there have been dated at 870 and 660 years old. The coast is dotted with such stone remains, mostly originating from within the last thousand years. By then the Namib had become increasingly arid, and uninhabitable even for the Bushmen. However, a Hottentot group of 'Strandlopers', or beachcombers, found a living on the coast itself from gathering seafish, white and black mussels and crayfish. Nowadays only strandwolves live in their stone circles, trying to keep out of the wind and flying sand, adding their seal-carcass remains to the heaps of mussel shells left by the humans who once shared their life and then decided to leave them to it.

We descended to the sea by means of a slipface scattered with white mussels dropped by gulls hoping to break them. In front of us the Atlantic waves, to the side sand cliffs. We were fortunate to find such an easy way down to the beach, for this was the Lange Wand. Walls of sand bearing down, cutting off.

There was no time to gaze about, taking in the scene. The tide was low – and still going down, we both agreed. If we were going to get along the Lange Wand – and where else was there to go? – now was the time. Tommy and I did a quick reconnoitre on foot, leaving the camels unattended – they wouldn't hurry back into those dunes. Tommy said he thought there were two problems. First, the foam formed by dead plankton, which rode the surf and would frighten the camels. Second, the rocks protruding from the beach sands – they were often masked by the foam and were sharp and slippery.

We calculated that there were 35 kilometres of Lange Wand ahead, perhaps less. It wasn't quite certain how we'd manage it before the tide came in again, but we agreed to give it a go – right away. This was the dangerous side to Tommy – the side that would take risks, the side that needed watching, but which I most admired. He told Henog that he must try to follow us with the Land Rover, but only when and where he thought it safe. For now he must stay right here – the camels might refuse to take even one step. Adrian could come along on foot to photograph if he liked, on condition that he kept himself ready to help us – or the Land Rover – when things got tough.

The wind screamed, the waves raced. Tommy led all three camels off and I walked behind, whirling a rope – this was no time for Andries to play. The beach was, as yet, at least 10 metres wide, and though Nelson almost seemed to be tiptoeing he was continuing quite steadily – not happy with the wind or the sea, but progressing nonetheless. Fifteen minutes of walking – Adrian already lost behind somewhere – and we were now beyond the first possible obstacle, a level shelf of wet black rock. Not much of a feat, but I was suddenly so proud of my camels. All those weeks in the Kalahari, the weeks since – through towns, trees, dunes – culminated in this test. And they were holding their nerve.

Two hours later we rounded a headland, wondering what was going to open up ahead of us. Kelp gulls [southern black-backed gulls] ripping at a dead Cape fur seal. White-fronted plovers speeding along the surf line. A party of swift terns attacking a fish shoal. So far the beach was still quite wide, letting us through. Another hour went by. Then a big wave confirmed a thought in my mind: the tide was on the turn.

Tommy was thinking the same. We still had no idea where we might escape from it if we didn't reach the end. We must hurry up – ride the camels, and trot.

Together, Tommy and I got the camels to sit down by shouting and waving the rope around, not putting up with any messing about. Then we were moving off, Andries walking free, behind. Things were fine until the first waves skidded up over the sands towards us – white foaming aggression which died away only just short of the sand slope. The waves soon crashed louder, racing at us. Finally, they were skidding in front of our eyes, cutting into the dune wall, curling around the camels' feet. Nelson, ahead of me, was shying. Jan, seeing Nelson panic, hopped a little up the sand wall, taking me with him. Andries was already up there.

For a moment, the waves were gone again. The camels, not knowing that the sea would be back, settled themselves and carried on. Then the flat, fast waves shot in at us again like living predators, carrying foam which they spat out lividly. Jan again tried to scramble up the wall. His legs were trembling – I could feel them beneath me. I saw that Nelson had turned around, and Tommy was tussling with him. Another wave, and Jan, eyes rolling, leaned to his side, pressing against the wall. In a moment, we were going to be cut off altogether. The waves weren't high, but they were very fast and strong.

There was nothing to do but get off the camels and run with them. I led – they'd have more faith in me – and Tommy jogged behind, scaring them with the rope. Ahead, 2 or 3 kilometres away, there was a cape, and as we came nearer we saw that waves were snugly fitting against it. The sea was already blocking our way.

But there was still reasonable hope that we could find a place above the tideline in one of the bays in between. We pressed on and finally rounded a corner. Here the beach widened out and above a lagoon, up a shallow slope, was a storm beach of mussel shells. We'd be safe there for the night. We remounted and let the camels walk at their own pace into safety. When we were at last in the peace of the lagoon, Nelson decided he'd had quite enough for today. He sat down in the water, and very professionally tipped Tommy off.

The vehicle still hadn't come through. Adrian turned up and together he and I waited with the camels, sitting behind them to avoid the wind, while Tommy went back along the beach. An hour passed. Maybe more. From time to time we looked out at the lagoon edge, where a strandwolf had died with its mouth open at the waterline, as if drinking salt water in desperation.

The Land Rover appeared only at last light, the engine now letting out a gravelly roar. 'We were almost stuffed,' Tommy announced, tumbling out of the driving seat. He was wet and bedraggled, like a wind-tossed lifeboatman. He explained that a wave had caught the vehicle and dragged them seaward. They had fought to get the engine started again while the waves came and went, washing around them. They had battled with the fading battery, taken out the plugs. Another wave had hit them. There was an explosion – the force of the water against the underside. They thought they were going to roll. And all the while the sand was sucking in the wheels. I could imagine the great hunk of a man keeping his nerve, sticking to his job, the waves spitting, the Land Rover keeling, until at last they got the engine to turn over. He ploughed the Land Rover out through the surf, staying in reverse gear until he was home and dry. Now Tommy was shaking as he told the story. 'I'm glad you didn't witness how scared I can be.'

**28 September**

We had a lazy morning, waiting for low tide at 11.40 a.m. The camels were saddled, the camp packed up, and we just waited, watching the sea. Some 10 kilometres more of Lange Wand lay ahead. Then we were ready. Tommy tried to start the Land Rover – and found its battery was dead. The morning passed as we tried to push the vehicle up and down the soft sand. Nothing.

The camels, meanwhile, got bored and wandered off. Later I found them down by the beach, paddling in the shallows. Nelson had dug himself deep into the seaside sand and looked like a middle-aged sunbather. He'd decided he quite liked the Skeleton Coast after all.

Back to the Land Rover. We tried digging furrows to ease its passage, raising the vehicle on a jack and spinning the wheel with rope, cooking the spark plugs in a casserole dish.

Genuinely trying to be helpful, I said, 'Of course, we could try to get the camels to pull the Land Rover out.'

Tommy was red in the face from pushing and sweat was raining down his beard. He turned to me, visibly fuming. 'You'd love that, wouldn't you? You've been waiting to say it for days.'

I'd been waiting to say it for weeks.

'I've a suggestion,' said Adrian, breaking in tactfully. 'But it's a last resort.'

'Go on …' said Tommy.

'Yes,' I said, 'you're the mechanic.'

'I can piss into the battery. It should give a little more life to it.'

'You're right,' Tommy said. 'That is a last resort.'

I suggested we put the battery in the sun to heat it up. So, on the most deserted coast in Africa, we sat sunbathing with the Land Rover battery – a camel's white feeding bowl beside it as a heat reflector. I began looking through my notes for the story of the *Dunedin Star*. It's a similar tale of inappropriate technology.

The cargo ship was holed on the night of 29 November 1942, 30 kilometres north of Cape Fria, while carrying twenty-one passengers and eighty-five crew. The captain decided to abandon ship, but after three trips to the beach in heavy seas their only motor launch was a write-off. The beach party, which included a heavily pregnant woman and three babies, had no shelter and was now cut off. Worse, when the rescue ships turned up two days later they could get through the waves only to those still left on the ship. The castaways were now alone.

An overland convoy of eight vehicles set out from Windhoek. At the same time, a Ventura bomber flew up from Cape Town to parachute supplies to the beleaguered party – and the aircrew were surprised to see that one of the retreating rescue vessels, the *Sir Charles Elliott*, had also struck the coast. Furthermore, while their twenty-man crew were trying to abandon ship a wave had swept away their only lifeboat, carrying it ashore with three men. The Ventura carried on up the coast to the *Dunedin Star* wreck and decided to land on the sand and gravels. Here, it got hopelessly stuck. The castaways – the passengers and forty-two crew – were now joined by the airmen.

Meanwhile, the crew of the *Sir Charles Elliott* tried to land another party ashore in a frail dinghy. It very soon capsized. Three men reached the land, while a fourth was swept away north, never to be seen again. More aircraft came and went, one of them to look for the overland convoy – of which nothing had been heard since their departure for the desert six days before. A second convoy set out to rescue them from the sands. At the *Sir Charles Elliott* wreck, three men rashly decided to swim for shore. All of them made it to the beach, where one immediately died of exhaustion.

The survivors were, in the end, lifted out bit by bit via air, sea and land, members of the original overland rescue convoy making the final part of the journey to the *Dunedin Star* on foot. The last of the castaways arrived in Windhoek on Christmas Eve, twenty-six days after the ship had run aground. But the misadventures didn't end there: a new convoy went to salvage the stranded Ventura. After enduring a nine-day journey to the coast, they got to work on the plane. When it took off the convoy turned for home, its mission accomplished. However, not long into the flight one of the bomber's engines seized. The plane plunged into the ocean, sinking with the crew inside. Then the Ventura's engines broke off and the aircraft bobbed up to the surface again. The two crewmen floated ashore in the fuselage. They had survived, somewhat miraculously, but now found themselves sitting without supplies on the Skeleton Coast. Their only hope was to intercept the retreating convoy. They must have been weak and in shock but they raced through the Namib sands, out of sheer desperation managing to cover 50 kilometres in time to meet up with the retreating salvage party.

And here we are, also marooned. The afternoon wind is blowing up – the sand stinging our cheeks, lips, eyes. We can't easily open our mouths to speak.

*Later:* soon after writing the above, we tried the Land Rover with the warmed-up battery. This time, success. We sprang into action, to leave before the waters cut us off again. But it was too late. Looking up the coast, we could already see the waves against the sand walls. Tomorrow, then.

### 29 September

We waited for the tide to turn, edging up the beach as far as we could. A baby seal emerged from the surf, startling the camels. It came right up and snuggled against my boot. The seal was weak, and had perhaps lost its mother in the currents. It was as if it wanted comfort. Lucky for him that I wasn't a jackal.

As we moved on, colonies of Cape cormorants skittered away over the surf, their wings touching the waves. The sea retreated, we made headway and a few hours later the Lange Wand sands began to lower, dropping down like calming seas, until we could at last see beyond them. A feeling of release.

We climbed on the camels and trotted on, then cut inland towards the Fishersbrunn outpost where Achim Lenssen would be meeting us to drop off the lucerne bales. 'He's always on time,' Tommy said, actually looking at his watch.

As we rode towards the outpost, Jan lagged further and further behind. I was battling even to keep him up to Nelson's plodding pace. Coming through salt bush or 'brackbush', the scrubby little pioneer plant that's his favourite, he walked right on by. The first edible vegetation for 320 kilometres, and he didn't see it. He'd given up looking.

# 6

# NO WOOD
# FOR THE COFFINS

*Evening:* have reached Fischersbrunn, the lonely Namdeb station. We feel dazed, stunned by the wind. Found a water tank and stood under its tap. Couldn't rub my face to clear the sand – sand grains scratched my wind-torn face.

A strange, deserted outpost. Winds howl, doors flap. As if to comfort themselves, people who've sheltered here have collected relics around them – ox horns, whale bones. The birds have done the same, gathering up fishing nets to nest in.

Achim drove up in his car, exactly on time. How can a man keep a rendezvous so precisely in a desert? I notice that one of his tyres is completely shredded. 'Had a puncture back there,' he said, shaking my hand. Also mentions he 'almost went down in quicksand' crossing the salt pan. This man has acquired a colossal reputation. The only person who drives out in the Namib-Naukluft alone, and yet he's missing a hand. The surgeon could have saved 'more than that' – I imagine a thumb's worth or more – but Lenssen wanted it all off. It was like a clean start. 'Look, man, it would just get in the way.' We made a fire in the shelter of a shed, and Achim puffed at his pipe and expounded his opinions, of which he has one on everything.

### 30 September, 34 kilometres north of Fischersbrunn
North, over quartz gravel plains laid on a fine sand. The camels negotiated a

*Tommy leading as we make our way through the high dunes towards Sandwich Bay. Andries had craftily chucked off his saddle again, but was reined in by me. Within days I would be progressing alone with the camels, and his antics were no longer quite so amusing.*

prickly surface of calcified reed stalks, dated (I've read) at 11,000 years old. These freshwater plants are a few metres above the present groundwater level – more evidence of the desert drying out.

We are following an 80-kilometre pipeline, now often reduced to splinters by the corrosive salt pans. The pipe was once a life-line, delivering (fairly) fresh water from Fischersbrunn to the outlying diamond fields, which date from soon after Stauch's discovery in 1908. Precious water also arrived in huge barrels trundled along like cricket pitch rollers by oxen – which were eaten on arrival.

Now we're camped in the lee of a huge crescent dune. The evening misty, and calm. Achim is excited by the weather – excited by a dull, overcast night. Puffs on his pipe, scratches his beard. An old sea salt. 'Man, it can really blow here … '

### 1 October, 'Conception Pump', 37 kilometres north of last position

North through Charlottenfelder, Holsatia and Conception, mining camps abandoned, like those in the rest of the Namib Naukluft, in the 20s and 30s. These quartz sands had been worked down to the granite bedrock. But the winds are working to undo the sand heaps and put the landscape back together again. At Holsatia, forty-three (I think it was) diamond- sorting trommels lying in a row, now choked by the sand they once sieved. A thicket of shovels stands beside them – perhaps fifty handles waiting to be grasped again. Elsewhere, sleeping quarters in triangular bunkhouses like chicken coops. A storeroom, spare parts still laid out, though the roof and walls have blown away. A mule shoe, bottles worn wafer-thin by the windborne sands. A graveyard ripped open by the winds. No gravestones, no coffins. Skeletons are spilling out of the sacks in which the corpses were laid. Skulls lie about casually, like washed-up fishing floats. A green stain around one man's wrist bone, indicating that a copper bracelet had decayed there with the flesh. Ironically, harsh though the desert is, the decay is slow – a lack of bacteria. One man, presumably one of the Ovambo labourers, still wears his hair – now like a woolly winter cap. There are also some straps of black skin on his bones, clinging like leathery seaweed.

Backing away, trying to show some semblance of respect, I tripped over a skull, knocking out three teeth. Appalled at myself. But is this any worse than nature does? No respecter of the weak, no respecter of the dead. A sudden pang – my mother, also taken away before her time.

Now we are at the old pumping station, Conception Bay. I'm using a whale vertebra as a stool. A foul smell like drains here – the old, trapped, sulphurous water from the flats. Around us in heaps, old bottles left by lonely men. And among the decaying metal gadgets, buckets and buckles, a camel's skull.

### 2 October, still at 'Conception Pump'

This morning, thickish mist. Took the camels 10 kilometres seaward to investigate the wreck of the *Eduard Bohlen*, a ship which ran aground in 1909 while bringing in supplies for the prospectors. As we left, Achim told us to be careful. Many vehicles have been lost in the salt pans, not least this one. 'Takes about an hour,' he said. 'Slow but steady. Sucks on the base of the vehicle.'

The sea has retreated over the years, the wreck now half a kilometre from the beach and propagating a dune. The decaying hull is lined with generations of bird and seal bones brought by strandwolves and jackals. Their tracks could be seen leading to and from the portholes.

Damara terns – diminutive, swallow-sized birds – arched about above us as we looked around. The jackals came home, their alert eyes a burning gold. We headed home ourselves, coming back across the salt pans, the salt beneath our feet divided into flat, angular plates.

Suddenly, a commotion behind. Tommy shouted, 'Quicksand!' I turned to see Nelson's eyes white with fear, his rear legs were sinking away out of sight. A strange phenomenon – the ground all of a sudden behaving like soup. Tommy was at his most authoritative: 'Keep moving! Keep moving!' Nelson yanked out his legs, powered by sheer terror. Afterwards we stood on the edge of the pan, collecting ourselves. Nelson was shaking. 'We almost lost him,' said Tommy, and Nelson let him hug his neck.

### 3 October

We've made 52 kilometres' progress, the furthest yet in a day. Now we are starting to feel the approach of the end, Walvis Bay. Everyone else is victorious but I'm sad – the elements running around loose out here are frightening but exhilarating.

Jan, just like the Land Rover and now Achim's Ford, which has 'alternator problems', is daily more resentful. When it comes to saddling time he curls his lip, snarling. Andries copies, making an unpleasant face like a thwarted Snoopy.

We trotted along a second, shorter Lange Wand. Cape fur seals sometimes lay asleep, many of them females soon due to bear young. Others were pups, and lay curled like car tyres. As we startled them they let out a snort and lolloped to the surf. Others did not move. Coming nearer, we found they were headless. The strandwolf finds the seal's brain a delicacy.

Above us sooty terns, swift terns, Sandwich terns, common terns. Ahead, seals in the surf, wriggling tadpole masses, and another wreck, the *Shawnee*, blocking our way.

*Below:* Shovels standing in the sand at Holsatia diamond settlement, north of Charlottenfelder, left just as they were when, in the Depressions of the 1920s and 30s, the miners of the Naukluft abandoned the desert and their dreams.

*Right:* Walking across the salt pans on a detour to the Eduard Bohlen *wreck. On the return journey the crust broke under Nelson and he was suddenly in quicksand. That we didn't lose him was largely thanks to the horsemanship skills of his rider, Tommy..*

**4 October, 37 kilometres done, south of Sandwich Bay**
*Morning:* I walk about before the others are up, happy to be alone in the crystal light of the early day, wondering what it will be like after Walvis Bay – whether my mind will be strong enough. For the moment I find peace and beauty here. For the moment I am able just to accept the desert, not question it. Then Achim wakes, combs his hair meticulously, almost strand by strand, and begins a logical analysis of the world. Unusual tide flows … Siltation in Sandwich Bay …

And it's all the worse because I suppose he represents a part of me that I'm trying to quash – the rationalizing, questioning side that's at the heart of Western culture, the driving energy of its researchers and 'explorers'. Whenever I've been with tribal people I've tried to learn how we can accept, not rule, 'nature' – but I, for one, am only a little changed. Achim, Tommy, Henog, Adrian and I need to be sent to the 'Bushmen', or the Himba at least, for more schooling. The whole of the Western world does …

*Later:* Jan slower than ever after yesterday's hard haul. As we turned inland, around Sandwich Bay, the dunes rose up ahead of us. And fell, and rose again. These were very new dunes, the sands unsorted, and therefore soft. The strain on the camels increased. We faced a wet salt pan. Nelson was well ahead now, I could see his footprints disappearing before my eyes. Jan slowed further. I cajoled, I threatened with a rope whip. But soon Andries, normally walking free at the back, was overtaking us. Jan picked up, scared at being left behind, then faltered again. And finally sat down. He had had enough. He rolled, dropping me off.

I was amazed – it had been so easy to get rid of me, yet he had chosen not to all these weeks. He trotted off to catch up the others, but even standing there abandoned on a salt pan I couldn't help but admire him. His loyalty up to now.

I walked the next 10 kilometres, following Jan's tracks, and ascending some low yellow dunes found Tommy with the others looking out over the bay. The water was calm, speckled with flamingoes. Others flew over in clouds, swinging like mass jet-fighter formations, pink and white. This is a vital staging post for the greater and lesser flamingoes. There are no breeding colonies here – access is too easy for jackals, and tides might drown the nests – so in December they head inland to Etosha and the lakes of Botswana.

Tommy and I herded the camels around the southern edge of the bay through what turned out to be a very difficult dune field. Often the lee slopes dropped at 38 degrees, sand's maximum angle of repose. The camels had to be coaxed to the edge, and there they peered over, resisting all efforts to make the descent but finally skiing down on all four flat feet.

To our left, dolphins cut through the water; jellyfish [this species, a first recording for the S.E. Atlantic] like maroon balloons turned in the surf. Flamingoes on the lagoon edge, dab, dabbing, stepping through the water. Running the beach, turnstones, dabchicks, African black oystercatchers. Cutting the breeze, Damara terns and Sandwich terns. We passed an inlet of *Phragmites australis* reeds and then the black iron ribs of the *Eagle*, beached here in 1861. Built in the United States in the 1830s, this early iron-hulled ship traded guano and probably also the fish that were dried on racks in the bay. Now it's nothing more than a rack itself.

Onward, me in front, Tommy behind, surmounting and descending dune after dune … As the camels skied down, they sometimes began mini-avalanches. The sands here were so well sorted they had exactly the same resonance when rubbed together. The effect of thousands of grains cascading in harmony was to send out a rumbling, sometimes a roar – the 'roaring dunes' often talked of by travellers.

*Dusk:* as I unsaddled Jan, he was particularly obtuse. He is ailing. Walvis Bay is 27 kilometres away. Tommy extra-hearty, either because we've pulled off the feat or because we're in reach of enough water to spare for a wash. A shower will, I admit, be pleasant. But tomorrow we shall be at Walvis Bay – centre of the lucrative fishing industry, exit point for Namibia's uranium, tin, copper, salt. All of this and more, after we've been in a place which feels as empty as the moon. Already I can feel myself braced for impact.

### 5 October

This morning, as I pottered about, making tea, dressing my sores, enjoying the desert's calm before the camp awoke, I saw there was something wrong with Jan. His eyes blue icy cool. And just now when I went to put the saddle on he snapped round as if to bite me. Carefully I felt his back with my fingers, and located a saddle sore between his shoulders.

*Later:* Tommy rode on Nelson, I dragged Jan by foot. Henog and Adrian drove off to Walvis Bay to alert the riding stables.

The first sign of the town was a car track, which slowly consolidated into a road. Ahead, brilliant hillocks of whiteness – the town's saltworks. Further up the coast, still wrapped in mist, the dockside cranes. We approached along the lagoon. The pans here were maroon and red – the algae having concentrated with the salt harvest as the water evaporated off. To our right, as we came to the town outskirts, were various man-made and plant defences against the advancing dunes, sands which were finally defeated when they met a string of classy bungalows – 'Millionaires' Row'. Tommy dismounted – we were now a traffic hazard. As we walked on by with the camels the black gardeners stood staring on the lawns – their hoses forgotten, wetting their boots. Road workers parted. A traffic

*Passing the* Shawnee, *a wreck from the mid 1970s. A tug converted to a trawler, it was on its way east for a refitting when it was abandoned to the infamous coast.*

control man with a red flag was pushed aside as Nelson strode on. Snappy little dogs snapped at gates, cars stopped dead in the road. Nelson paused, surveyed the shrub borders, eyed the juicy blossoms, approved, and kept walking.

Two press photographers were clicking away, well-wishers running up. I let Tommy lead into town, while I hid behind Andries. All these people taking such interest, being so warm, but it was all too overwhelming.

Then Achim began herding the camels with his Ford to keep the pace up. 'They're asleep!' he said, actually parking his vehicle, getting out and giving the camels a thrash with the rope. For the first time I wanted Jan to kick someone.

We cut behind Walvis Bay to the stables. The horses out in the paddocks pricked up their ears, trotted forward, tails stiffly out. Then they spun in the dust, electrified. A girl calmed her shying pony, braving the escape route past us. It wasn't very long before she retreated in disarray.

Mrs Kleyenstüber showed us to the camel quarters. Our attention turned instinctively to the leader, Nelson. Would he tolerate these small holding pens? Nelson looked around at the homely stalls, the awed children (each one a poten-

*Greater flamingoes (*Phoenicopterus (ruber) roseus*), taking off near Walvis Bay. Although this is not a breeding site, the population of greater and lesser flamingoes (*Phoeniconaias minor*) can number 40,000, the wading flocks joined by floating African white and pink-backed pelicans (*Pelicanus onocrotalus *and* P. rufescens*) and numerous stalking surf-line feeders.*

tial carrot donor), and approved. He walked into the first. We slotted the other two camels next door, where they'd still be able to touch each other.

John drove up in his camouflaged Toyota with Maria [his wife], and both dug into action, smoothly organizing Adrian and me, easing the shock – so many people talking to us, the outside world pressing us. Took us for a wash at their house, and gave us a mug of tea. We found ourselves babbling, a little incoherent.

Back to the stables – the vet had come to see Jan. I took Andries out of Jan's pen and went in by myself, not taking my eyes off him. He was nervous, and there was no room here to escape those legs. I firmly ordered Jan to sit. He hesitated, raised one knee, wondering – then obeyed. I hobbled both legs and told the vet, a wary Dr Rodenwoldt, that Jan was now secured and he could come in. The vet did enter, but was soon out again when Jan sprang up, breaking both hobbles. Next we used a spare timber to corner Jan against the kraal side poles.

Adrian heaved on Jan's lead rein, tightening it against a post. As Jan fought, the rein snapped … and snapped again. He spat viciously at me – the camel's famous, foul, vomity spray – and his legs began flying in wild curves, trying to catch me.

Suddenly, the situation was dangerous. I remember seeing the vet duck out of the pen. Alone with Jan, I saw that bully's look come into his face. If I backed out now he'd always remember – today, tomorrow, some time when we were alone in the desert. I knew I must stand my ground. I moved round the kraal sides, facing him, like an outclassed boxer evading an opponent. I remember talking to him, 'Jan, Jan …', and being amazed at how calm my voice sounded. Next, he had me trapped in the corner. 'That's *enough*, Jan.' He was right against me, his breath in my face, eyes crystal hard. He thought about it, half raising a knee to kick. I was pinned against the kraal, with one of my legs bent up to fend off blows. Suddenly he flashed a knee into my chest, then another. Quick blows, a boxer moving in. Then he stepped back.

'We only get one chance,' the vet said, once I'd recovered and we were about to try our next tactic. I thought, 'We've already had our chance.' This time I pushed Andries against Jan, using Andries' body to block him against the posts. Andries hasn't an ounce of spite in him, and as usual thought this was all a game. Jan bit him and he let out a squawk, but then rubbed his nose on Jan's cheek.

With Andries holding Jan in place the vet climbed up the kraal posts and looked down. A classic saddle sore was diagnosed and cleaned. Twice daily I have to apply an ointment. 'The camels need four or five days' rest,' he said.

As the vet packed his little bag of medicines, I looked at Jan. My fear is that he'll never go back to that ordinary, everyday bloke that he was – or that I thought he was.

Lenssen told Adrian: 'Benedict's going to see his arse.' Which means, I suppose, 'have a catastrophe'. Maybe this desert expert is right to be pessimistic. Alone, only one thing need go wrong – one broken girth strap, one fall.

Slept appallingly. Claustrophobic – closed off skies, imprisoned air.


### *6 October*

Tommy said his last words to the camels, talking to them one by one. 'Nelson, I'll miss your moans. You take care of the others for me, right?' Then Andries. 'Shit-head. You've got to grow up to be a good camel, yeah?' He turned to Jan. 'And Jan …' Well, there weren't many nice things anyone could say about Jan.

Tommy said to me, softly, 'I'm worried. About the next stage … .' He clearly wanted to get something off his chest.'Water is my main concern.' Having said that, he gave a monologue on the threat of rhinos, which he knew well, having pioneered with Rudi Loutit the dehorning programme to confound poachers. 'Rhinos will run at your camp fire. They're attracted to the light.'

'Right. I mustn't light camp fires,' I said. No great problem there.

On the other hand, he went on, in elephant and lion country fires were essential. 'And sleep near a steep hill, which you can escape up.'

I remembered a Himba settlement I had seen near Porrus. They'd built extra huts on the hill, a retreat for when the elephants passed through.

'And if a lion attacks?'

'If you're charged by a lion, I wouldn't fire until it's on you. Whose gun are you taking?' I told him that the pilot André Schoeman, who'd helped fly me about on my recces, had promised to lend me his revolver.

'Put a wrap, a jacket, around your least important hand, say your left, and let the lion take it. Put the barrel into the lion's mouth and fire.' He spoke matter-of-factly, as if this was daily routine. But how do you put a wrap around your hand with a lion charging you? 'Or,' he continued, 'use that big knife of yours, and go for just above the ribs. Don't waste time with the neck. It's all muscle.'

This wasn't very encouraging last-minute advice to get from another distinguished Namib expert. 'And sleep against a boulder, to shield my head?' I asked.

'That you should do anyway, as a matter of course.'

Having ladled out copious instructions on how to deal with all these species, Tommy couldn't think of any advice at all to give me about the camels. 'If you hobble them, a lion might just try to take one. If you don't, they'll wander.'

With his final goodbyes he said, 'As you know, Nelson is the camel who'll get you out of trouble, if you need to go for help.' It's very true. Below me is a vast pyramid of contacts, dozens of people who've been good enough to help me along. But in the end it all comes down to a camel called Nelson.

### 8 October

Jan still tetchy, swiping his long jaw at my arm to bite at it. An old German buffer came to look at the camels and reminisce. 'In the First World War my father had camels – the fastest way of getting help from a neighbour.' He remembered vividly the Camel Corps riding by one day. A black had his head bitten off.

'Are you absolutely sure? Perhaps as a boy it just seemed like that.'

'The head was left hanging by a flap. It stuck in my memory.'

He walked away, leaving me to picture the unhappy, though interesting, scene.

I took the camels off to graze. This was their first-ever really green field. I had to teach them how to eat the soft grass, plucking each mouthful for them. Despite all they've been through, they are still so innocent in the ways of the world.

# 7

# THE MISTS
# OF BRANDBERG

**12 October**

What does the town consist of? Cosy Bay (a half-hearted coffee shop/restaurant), an ironmonger, Woolworths … There is more, but the above list is symptomatic. Walvis Bay is simply a junction – for cars, ships, fish. 'Bit of a dump,' people from the capital say. Perhaps that's why I like it.

It has no need to cater to the whims of the idle tourist – a creature all-powerful in most of Africa. Its eyes are firmly elsewhere, out to sea. The ocean is where it makes a living – the cargoes to be gathered in or dispatched. So when the wind blows south, the town is cloaked in fishy smells. If the wind doesn't blow from inland, mist creeps in. Either way, trains clank at the docks regardless. Want entertainment? Better to try Swakopmund, the old German town up the coast. In Walvis Bay you get the Plaza Disco – under-aged girls, pole-axed men. Otherwise, there's … well, that's all there is. And if you want to stay in to watch a video, get to the video hire shop by 5 p.m. or your choice will have gone.

However, even since my reconnaissance trip all this has begun to change. Walvis Bay is no longer an 'island', a port kept on by South Africa for strategic and economic reasons; it's now becoming aware of its new place within Namibia. Land is being snapped up, lawns being laid over the desert. The Cosy Bay restaurant is revamping its fried-food menu, updating its muzak. You can now buy a pizza at Crazy Mamas. The pornographic shop, until this year in someone's garage, has now proudly taken its place near the Shopping Mall.

*Leaving Kuisebmond, the black 'location', or township, on the edge of Walvis Bay.*

### 13 October

Final preparations. Jan judged fit. I have made a point of handling him as much as possible, readying him for D-Day. The feet of all the camels are in excellent condition. As I'd always hoped, the sand of the south has worked them into thick, crusty pads. Went to Swakopmund to collect the revolver from André Schoeman. He landed on the airstrip – seemed to me like just a marked-off bit of desert – and, as if in a car, drove up to the lone petrol pump for refuelling. 'It's a pea-shooter,' he said, handing the gun over, 'but it should scare most things.'

'And rounds of ammunition?'

'Enough to start a small war.'

André's wife, Jeanita, will probably buy the camels at the end of the journey. When she met them a couple of days ago at the stables they took an instant liking to her. She put her head to Jan's teethy jaws – yet he spared her.

### 14 October

Emergency. Günter Kock, who's been brilliant in all he's done so far, has had to pull out. As it stands, there is no one to place my supply depots. I'm heading into the desert with no food and only a few freshwater springs out there. Rapid reassessment with the help of John and his never-ending web of contacts. The grazing, which has been so exceptional this year because of comparatively heavy rains, still seems to be lasting. Our feeling is that, given my existing depots at the Schoemans' Fly-In Safari camps at Huab and Purros, and a bit of additional help from depots placed by Adrian with John and his trusty Toyota, I'll make it. But more warnings by phone from both Achim and Tommy, who want me to take a radio 'at least'. I won't – I still insist I know my strengths and weaknesses. However, under the weight of so much expert opinion – only the Schoeman brothers seem optimistic – Adrian's doubts must be growing.

### 16 October

Day of departure, and John's trusty Toyota has broken down. Still, he has time to repair it. It'll take me days to get to Henties Bay, the final settlement before the pure desert. Meanwhile Adrian and John will occasionally monitor my progress in another vehicle – we aren't yet sure if the camels will follow me when I'm truly alone. Certainly from now on I won't be riding. Stuck up in the air on a camel you feel surprisingly out of touch with your surroundings. Besides, if I'm thrown, no one will cart me off to hospital.

After the constrictions of a town, a feeling of liberation. The camels felt the same. They were out of their tight pens and so was I. We virtually ran for freedom

– I'm afraid we caused mayhem among the horses as we left. Pounding of hooves, panting, prancing, and in the paddock, horses and their riders ploughing through the jumps.

Adrian and I hoiked the camels around the back of the town, through the reeds of the bird sanctuary, and across a main road and back down to the beach. This took me right beside Kuisebmond, a black township which everyone calls 'the location'. Not a bad place – low, tightly packed, pastel houses parked tight against the dunes. And whereas any whites seeing me had just wound down their car windows and started taking snaps, the blacks ran over to us and shouted out with glee. The children shrieked, skipped and jumped along behind, their legs flying in the sand. Their whoops attracted more children. And more.

We now had to cut through a back street. The children were pressing in, their voices echoing off the walls. I thought the camels were going to lose their nerve. They'd panic, kick out. We passed a large yellow tent I recognized, the Assemblies of God church, and the flapping canvas upset the camels further. I became scared. The children were shrieking, ducking around and about the camels' legs. Would a child survive a kick in the head? I hardly dared think of it. I looked about for help. Jan looked around, his eyes hateful. I tried to talk to him. But he was already beyond hearing, and a madness was raging in him. In the end he was triggered by a youth screaming up behind on a bicycle. Jan jolted forward, knocking me in the thigh with one of his famous knees. Pain, but I held on to the three reins. What else could I do – let three frightened camels loose among three hundred children?

The housing stopped abruptly and we were out in the dunes. But the crowds didn't diminish – they grew. Now the adults were running behind as well, wanting to know where their children were going. The whole lot streamed out over the sands. Five hundred? Six hundred?

At dusk we were still being followed through the sands. Now there were only six children and one of them was crying because he was hungry and tired. I told them they must go back now. But they turned away only when it was approaching last light.

### 17 October

Late start as I rearranged the supplies each camel takes in the canvas bags. My food from now on: dried milk and muesli for breakfast, dried fruit for the day, cans of cooked meat and beans for night-time – cans as a safety measure because bolting camels will break packets, and maybe water containers. Also because at night the wind will be at its strongest and I might not be able to light my gas

*Kaiser Wilhelm Street, Swakopmund. In 1892 the Germans erected a makeshift landing stage on the empty shore to facilitate the arrival of soldiers and settlers to their new acquisition. Although South Africa overran the colony soon after, in 1915, the town still retains an atmosphere of the old Fatherland.*

stove – all food must be pre-cooked.

It wasn't long before we approached the town of Swakopmund, a bit of left-over Germany. Houses not crouching as they did at Walvis Bay but imposing themselves on you across wide, clean streets. Gables, turrets, stucco and other extravagances, grand and formal adornments in the Jugendstil or Art Nouveau style that was fashionable before the First World War. A little self-important? Yes, but charming, the buildings like the follies of eccentric and self-indulgent millionaires. It pleased the camels to walk between the regimented flowerbeds of this

oasis, and pleased me to see the gaping faces of Germans in cafés, as they dropped their pastries. So long now since their grandfathers were handling their own camels out here. In the very first days, before the jetty was built, the ships importing camels to the colony simply threw them overboard to swim ashore. Later it was better organized; the camels came to shore one by one, dangling upside-down from cranes. And then off the bewildered creatures went to be fashioned into smart members of the Camel Corps.

Traffic police sped to my aid, as arranged. Then, as I was about to negotiate the town centre along Kaiser Wilhelm Street, they sped off for their lunch break. Everyone was very understanding as the camels spread themselves, blocking cars in and out. We were always first away from the traffic lights, but they had always changed again before we'd got across the junctions. Andries held us up further by stopping and making mooing noises, the plaintive sound that Skerpioen used to make back at the farm to call the other animals back. Andries, though, was simply looking at his own reflection in a shop window.

Adrian reappeared and we made our way to the farm of Mrs Erb, the German woman whose family included eight camels. In the course of the reconnaissance trips she had given me many tips and I wanted her to see the camels she'd enabled me to train with gentleness. Nelson's mouth actually gaped when he saw Mrs Erb's camels. He strode forward, throthing excitedly at the mouth. His tail began flapping rhythmically. And he began urinating, the tail swishing it everywhere. 'A typical male greeting,' Mrs Erb said, as Nelson barged by. Andries mooed, Jan too tried to urinate. It was a happy scene.

After a while, though, Jan seemed uneasy about Nelson's sudden switch in loyalty from his group and tried with his neck to peel Nelson away. Nelson wouldn't be moved. He had now blown up the mouth bladder that camels are equipped with especially for impressing each other. It spilled out, a revolting pink mass dripping with saliva. Andries, meanwhile, had found his own friend, Dollar, a little female of about his age.

We led my camels around to a side paddock and housed them out of reach of the others for the night. Elke Erb made us a pot of potatoes and cabbage, which we ate surrounded by a million camel effigies – camel carvings, emblems, paperweights, photos, silhouettes. While Adrian nodded off, she and I talked until late about camels, their great strengths and also their one or two little weaknesses.

Tomorrow, my first day alone. When they realize it's desert they're heading into again, will the camels still agree to follow me?

### 18 October

**Dawn:** goodbye to Adrian, though he'll meet me on a few more occasions. John and he will bring horse pellets and water for the camels, plus my own food supplies which I've already bought and pre-packed in Walvis Bay, to points that I should reach (on the basis of my doing 25 kilometres a day) every ten days. The horse pellets that we'll carry will last only four days (5 kilos a day each) and the camels have to make up the other six with grazing. Various springs should provide the camels with water every week, at worst. One of Mrs Erb's camel workers, Tobias, will walk with me a short way to help me get my camels away from hers.

**Later:** off I went with Tobias' help, but an hour later Nelson and Andries were still moaning and mooing and looking over their shoulders, distressed at leaving the other camels behind. We continued through rolling hills of quartz gravels. At last, Tobias had to turn back. The camels watched him go, then turned around to look at me – then at the desert stretching into oblivion ahead. I stood facing them. They stood facing me. I was so vulnerable. And they mustn't know it.

I briskly tied Jan to the rear of Nelson's saddle, and Andries to the back of Jan. 'Come!' I said, trying to make it sound the most obvious thing in the world. They did come. I closed my eyes and smiled in relief.

Struck out north-north-east through white gravels and salt bush, using my compass from my top pocket. Checked my heading every fifteen minutes, and with the sun knew I was more or less lined up all right. Nothing much to fix a bearing on, but by noting first one distinguishing crease on the gravel horizon, then the next, I could make my way along a fairly straight course.

At dusk I sat the camels down, hobbled them, gave them their horse-pellet supper and fixed my exact position in the middle of nowhere with the GPS. Then I made my camp, rolling out my sleeping bag behind a wind barrier of saddles and opening up the food department in my bags. To my horror, all I could seem to find for supper was meatballs. I suddenly remembered: at the supermarket in Walvis Bay I'd been seduced by a special offer. Must remember to tell Adrian to unpack all my other supply boxes waiting in Walvis Bay, and get him to swap the meatballs for something more edible than gristle with mud gravy.

Checked the camels' hobbles again as I brushed my teeth. Don't think I'll sleep for the fear of them abandoning me. I did once actually buy the camels beautiful shiny cow bells, so I could locate them. But Tommy said, 'Well, the lions will be grateful. They love to hunt down cattle with bells on.'

Now bedtime. I'm lying under the stars, a little paraffin lamp to write by. The camels parked as a windbreak. I'm damp and chilly even lying in my sleeping bag with an insulating mat beneath, and wearing long johns and jumper. But full of optimism. The most beautiful prospect, this journey. If I can maintain control of the camels, and of myself, I'm among the raw fabric of existence.

### 19 October

I did sleep, and woke just before dawn. The camels shuffled forward on their knees as I tipped the water container, sparing a trickle of water to brush my teeth. Shuffled even closer as I spared another trickle of water to wash my face. They know my routines, and try to befriend me whenever there's water or something tempting like muesli around.

*Overleaf: To ensure camel contentment, every time I sat the camels down I had to take great care to place Andries (centre) beside Nelson (right), whom he adored. The loyalty of my camel companions touched me again and again: not once in the six weeks we were alone in the desert together did I feel lonely.*

Up to now we've been walking over sharp desert gravels but today I passed over fields of them wearing lichen coats. The lichens had blunted the rock surfaces and rendered the place friendly. As I walked, they unfurled in the fog. Some types were crustose, lying flat on the delicate gypsum soils, while others were foliose, with little branches. Still others, like the one called *Xanthomaculina convoluta*, were in orange clumps and rolled along free, blown by the wind.

I rested at midday, and was about to let the camels feed on a salt bush when I spotted a horned adder lodged in it. An angry little animal, seeing three camel heads bearing down. It really hissed, like a cartoon snake, and struck viciously at my camera as I filmed. But even after that the camels couldn't spot it.

At dusk I got out the feeding bowls as usual and gave the camels their horse pellets, then made a half-igloo wind shelter with the saddles and bags and lit the gas stove to put on some tea. Among all the meatballs, I was delighted to find one tin of 'chicken piri-piri'. But it proved to be an extremely hot curry – hardly the thing for a man with blistered lips. So it's meatballs again, supplemented by baked beans, peas or sweet corn.

### *21 October*

Henties Bay. Last town. Kraai Krause and Patrick Eagleton, who run a bar called Myl 50, and (it seems) half of Henties Bay besides, were determined to give me a royal send-off from this, the final settlement. Stowed my camels safely away in their back yard with fresh hay, and me safely away in a free chalet. As much drink as I wanted at the bar and a vast platter of fresh crayfish. Almost expected to find a woman waiting in my bed – they'd thought of everything else.

John and Adrian came in the little van. The Toyota – which they'll need to bring me my supplies out to the rendezvous points – is still not fixed.

In the restaurant Adrian was agitated, not his usual reasonable self. For the first time ever we began raising our voices at each other. He thinks that, without the depots which were to have been placed by Günter Kock, and no radio communication, I'm still in grave trouble. He dropped a bombshell: 'I felt it was my duty to ring and warn Patrice [BBC Unit Manager].'

'I hope you didn't worry her,' I said, already sure he had.

'Actually, I told her it's only a problem if the BBC don't want the TV series to have a dramatic and bloody ending.'

'Thanks, Adrian,' I said. Didn't even he have faith in me? But I hated myself for being cross – he'd only done it because he was worried. And I'd been almost alone for four days, hadn't thought of the world outside, let alone its point of view. Whether I thought so or not, expert opinion was that my expedition might come to a sticky end.

Patrick Eagleton arrived at this point and inadvertently made things worse by entertaining us with a story of a lion attacking an elephant. He'd seen the carcass – its belly ripped clean open as it ran to escape. 'Here the lions have learnt to avoid maddened feet.'

I made reassuring noises to Adrian. I'd crossed the Amazon Basin, been through a lengthy New Guinea initiation ceremony. And now I'd trained a camel team from scratch in three weeks. But the truth is, my confidence is knocked. I know I seem like a dreamer to those who don't know me – people like Achim Lenssen, even fellow travellers and explorers. Perhaps, after all, that's what I am.

*Late at night:* John and Adrian have left. My fears? The desert itself presents problems, as it should. But my greatest obstacle is myself. Will I be mentally tough enough to withstand my own company, six weeks of seeing virtually no one, when all my hidden shadows and ghosts come out?

### 22 October
Goodbye service station, goodbye houses, goodbye road. Hello desert.

Walked out into nowhere, again attracting crowds of blacks from their 'location'. Children began cartwheeling behind us. A man wearing what looked like a pair of shiny paisley pyjamas walked alongside playing on a Fuji electric keyboard. At last my entourage began to lose interest. A child called Elvis instead ran after a lizard. The crowd joined the chase, until it was stamped dead, snuffed out like an ember.

Alone, the camels and I dropped out of the sea breeze, heading up the Omaruru River. As dry now as almost every Namibian river, its dusty bed was sometimes a kilometre wide. The air was still, the musky smells hanging in clouds. Some trees were flourishing from underground water, others were on their sides, smashed by flash floods, lying like broken-hearted cripples.

It's now midday and I feel free – I've mastered my little world. This is the liberty that a yachtsman must experience, the relief of casting off into open seas. You are God of your Universe. I lead, Nelson follows carrying two huge bags of essentials – the only camel sensible enough to be trusted with life-saving provisions such as food – and the solar panels. Andries follows, carrying my kitchen gear and my office. Jan walks in the rearmost position, carrying clothes and the horse pellets which, placed on his own back, are out of reach of his teethy mouth.

*Later:* after almost a day of this sweet stillness, the silence was interrupted by a stray car driving down the gravel bed. I waved it down. I thought the driver might kindly deliver a message to Kraai, giving my latest progress. The driver wound the window down. 'I have no time to talk. One of my passengers is a heart-attack victim.' The only car for perhaps weeks here, and it stops just to tell me it can't stop. 'We must get someone to hospital,' the driver explained. I glimpsed at the passengers as the car drove off. They all looked equally ill.

It's now evening. I'm on my own – but not in the slightest lonely. I'm happy just to be with the camels – Jan breathing noisily through his pegged nose, Nelson grizzling, Andries hobbled with one foot like the rest but hopping off into the dark, mooing at the others to come out and play. During the daytime, the camels have so far followed me without tugging. But the test will be when we are crossing difficult ground, or they are hungry or thirsty – or think they are heading into nowhere, which of course they are.

Having fed the camels and constructed a windbreak from the saddles, I usually fall asleep within moments. As I predicted, the wind is often too great by dusk to allow the gas stove, so I eat the ghastly meatballs uncooked, with a can of beans to ease them down. Then write, racing to get the words down before I succumb.

### 23 October, 20 kilometres north up track towards Strathmore Mine

Before we set foot anywhere each day, I face up to two hours of getting the camels ready – packing the food, rebottling the paraffin from the lamp, saddling the camels, loading the packs, strapping on the solar panels, making sure nothing is loose, no girth straps slack, nothing flaps. I wake before 5.30, when it's still dark. From that moment my eye is half on the horizon, measuring the progress of the sun. It's a race against the oncoming day. Further north, and inland, it will also be a race against the oncoming heat.

Quartz sands dazzle. Mist also dazzles. Mica chips flash like mirrors from these plains of rough-angled quartz. I wear the tablecloth over my face like a bandit, but I'm still burning – lips especially, despite zinc sunblock ointment that state-of-the-art cricketers favour, applications through the day of a stick of UV block, and my broad-brimmed hat. The sands bulge up and roll, as we push north to the deserted tin mine.

As I was eating my daytime snack – usually biscuits and dried fruit – heard a hissing by my feet. Froze. Snake? Camels looked to me – hadn't even heard it. I looked about, slowly, but couldn't see anything. This reminded me of the jungle, when you've been there a month and your sixth sense is suddenly telling you something is wrong. You cannot see what exactly, because all around there are leaves blocking your view. So you have to wait for whatever it is to betray itself by making a move. Here in the desert, I suppose I now also have a feeling for my surroundings, and at this moment found myself waiting in just the same way. And right in front of me my eye did, indeed, detect a movement. A fat lizard, rocking itself. I bent to look, and found it was a Namaqua chameleon, puffed up with air. It was the enamel colour of the quartz sand and in a state of near hysteria, one eye on the camels that were blocking out the sky and the other on me. As I peered, it swivelled its eyes and flashed open its pink and yellow mouth – a terrible display of anger.

Looking at this strange, other-worldly creature, I could see why the chameleon is seen in Africa as malevolent, a creature of sorcerers and doers of evil. The wonky, spherical eyes, with their tired, wrinkled, leathery lids, the creepy colour transformations, the toes splitting into two clasping branches, like tongs.

The chameleon had had enough, and plodded off at surprising speed with a stick insect's clockwork gait, tilting from side to side. It made its way towards the only cover, the camels. As it clambered up Nelson's leg, it became the burnt caramel colour of his coat. Nelson tolerated the chameleon's studied climb for a while, then flicked it off. It plodded over to Jan's leg. 'I shouldn't do that to Jan if I were you …' I mumbled. Too late. The chameleon was sent flying into oblivion.

I'm camped in the most shelter I can find – only a slight dent in this smoothly rolling landscape. It's dusk. Ahead, occasional rock lines, black lumps from a white quartz bed. A soft, female landscape, the flats giving rise to smooth, tawny mounds. And way, way out there, the magnificent Mount Brandberg, set like a shrine, bold but aloof on the horizon. As yet, only a smoky blue block – it's still far away. But already it's more than the sum of its parts. Already it is more than a mountain, more like some extension of the earth itself.

### 24 October, in riverbed 14 kilometres north-east of Strathmore Mine

Mist until midday. Birds invisible in it, twittering – larks perhaps. The light piercing. More undulating gravels, more black boulder lines, when suddenly I saw ahead of me the tracks of three camels and a human being … I stared, disbelieving. I had walked in a circle. Immediately I parked the camels and did a thorough investigation: this must *never* be allowed to happen again. Turned and retraced my steps, saw how I'd looped around – distracted, it seemed, by Nelson, who'd wanted to stop and destroy a bush. The horizon invisible – the quartz merging with the mist. At times, these are 'white-out' conditions. You cannot judge the ground – in fact you can't even distinguish it from sky. For the first time while

*Overleaf: The Brandberg at twilight. An awesome massif with a 2574-metre peak, the mountain is the highest in Namibia, dating from volcanic activity 120 million years ago. Since then, surrounding lavas have been eroded away, leaving this lump of weather-resistant granite.*

navigating, I got out my GPS to fix my position. Even had there been physical features to take a bearing from, compass and map navigation was out of the question – and it might be like this for the next week.

Now I'm in a riverbed where John and Adrian will meet me – if they've got the Toyota into action. Slightly anxious: Jan has kicked over a container, drowning my £500 Canon Eos and leaving me with only three days' water supply.

The camels and I are presently huddled together behind a bush. It provides limited shelter – Nelson has already chewed it thoroughly. I was tired when I arrived here, but for an hour I had to keep an eye on the camels as they grazed – it's said that many camels from the German days died from eating poisonous plants. Around me are gravels and occasional dollar plants, inedible succulents with thick coin leaves. Dried mud lies in parchment scrolls, animal prints preserved in it. They are a comforting sign of life. I look on them as friendly spirits.

My eyes feel strained – twelve hours of squinting. Snow blindness from these mica-rich sands is not unknown, and, for once, I donned sunglasses today.

So far, the camels' feet have held up well to the thumping and cutting of the ground. The worst is still a long way off. Nelson holds back sometimes, glimpsing the looming foothills. The Brandberg is hanging out there in the mist …

### 25 October

Still waiting for Adrian and John – I'm rationing my water now. Took the camels on a walk. They thought I was going to take them to some grazing, but I just wanted a close-up look at the plant called *Welwitschia mirabilis*. An unsightly heap really – it has two leaves which spring from a low cork disc, splitting into wide straps whose ends are shredded by the winds. Arguments still rage about its exact classification: part pine tree, part more advanced flowering plant, part club-moss. Its pollination is also a mystery, but probably takes place via wasps, whose leg hairs carry the sticky pollen grains between plants. The species is immensely slow-growing – the specimen I was looking at was perhaps 500 years old – and so doesn't draw too heavily on the desert's limited supply of nutrients. It has a huge tap root but can also absorb moisture through the leaves, which are fibrous and resist all but large grazers like rhino and gemsbok, which tackle it only when desperate. A red-legged, yellow-backed, black-spotted bug called *Probergrothius sexpunctatis* is usually to be seen walking about its underside and sucks sap from the plant. Unfortunately the reduviid [assassin] bug also resides there, and it enjoys sucking the juices of the poor old red-legged, yellow-backed, black-spotted bug.

Back at the camp. The Brandberg sits to the north-east like a burnt rusk, pounded, chipped, scarred, magnificent. Between 110 and 130 million years ago the mountain was a vast intrusion of granite, a lump of molten rock surrounded by volcanic lavas. Now the lavas have been weathered away, leaving a few humps of granite on the periphery for me to dodge, and The Brandberg itself. Nelson sits by me, waiting for refreshments. I have nothing to give him. His breath is sweet today – he's been eating grass. About half an hour ago Andries ran off, chased by a stick that got caught on his lead rein. I found him sitting beyond the horizon. He had trapped the stick under him as if it was a predator. I had some difficulty luring him back to the camp, and had to lead Jan and Nelson out of sight so that he'd think he'd been abandoned. He came back quickly enough then … This is how I maintain control of these powerful animals, by exploiting their insecurities.

The camels are gathered around me again, munching like the Three Witches in *Macbeth*. They are relaxed, I'm relaxed. I've noticed that we are developing similar rhythms of work and play. Have I compromised with them, or have they compromised with me? Certainly I walk more slowly now, dropping back to their pace. We are starting to work together, and I find I have energy to spare. It's no longer three against one.

*Later:* Adrian and John arrived as the dark fell. Not in the camouflaged Toyota but in the blue van, which now sounded as if it had lost its exhaust pipe. Relief, but also disquiet seeing them. I don't want to hear about the outside world. But Adrian tells me that there's a photo of the camels and me dominating the back page of *The Times*. He also says he's spoken again to the BBC. They've authorized rescue by vehicle/plane 'as and when necessary'. I should be relieved, but I couldn't care less. Whatever any experts say, I feel certain I will succeed here. Besides, no plane or vehicle will find me out in the desert. Not unless I carry a radio. But I make grateful noises – one day, when this is all over, I shall be thankful that Adrian really cares about me. I derive great comfort from his words: 'I've never met anyone like you, Benedict – your stamina, power of endurance.'

### 26 October

Marched off this morning towards that giant red rock, The Brandberg. Welwitschias from time to time … Nelson always stops to sniff them. Does he detect something aromatic and pleasing? Or is he simply delaying our progress as he used to on the dune crests, stopping to urinate extremely slowly to put off the tricky descent?

The stones are beginning in earnest. This is the first indication that we are entering Damaraland, and the eroded mountains created 850–500 million years ago. The granites, mica schists [mica presented in foliated layers of rock] and gneiss [a laminated rock of quartz, feldspar and mica] were ground down through

*Right:* The industrialized world prizes the Namib diamonds above all else. But also lying in the desert are the relicts of Bushmen – these etchings from Twyfelfontein. The Damaraland etchings and paintings, some 5000 years old, increasingly represent to us a lost time of harmony with natural resources – and may yet be valued beyond that of the diamond, literally the adamas or 'invincible' stone.

*Above:* The Namaqua chamelion (Chamaeleo namaquensis) is a terrestrial species, entirely adapted to life on the ground in hot and apparently desolate regions. It eats grasshoppers, beetles and even snakes, and buries its eggs in the sand. It is even known to forage on sea shores, a nasal gland allowing it to get rid of excess salt.

the aeons, leaving a mere stump, the Namib platform. We shall be passing over the centre of it, and now there are no sands to soften the rocks for the camels. For the present I can bypass them by following old watercourses, gravelly tongues that meander through the sparse grass slopes. Progressing like this leaves a feeling of supreme satisfaction. I use only 1: 250 000 maps – whole hill ranges go barely recorded at this scale – and I navigate by feeling my way through the forms of the land, searching out soft riverbeds and gentler slopes for the camels' sake.

Now we have passed into the foothill grasslands, the dying sun reddening the rock face of The Brandberg. To the north, the dark plateau which is Damaraland. I walked another 40 kilometres today, but feel utterly fresh. I feed off this ever-changing desert as it shuffles its features, transforms itself with soft and hard light. Wildlife is magnified by the emptiness. Gemsbok turn their emblazoned heads my way, their black and white masks watching as we go by. Springbok eat rapidly, always ready to run. When they do flee they wave their frail whip tails and pronk, as Afrikaners say – sail high through the air. It's so-called 'honest advertising', in this case showing predators they are fit – why not instead go for that incompetent antelope trailing at the back?

### 27 October

It's 6 a.m. Camels have been fed (horse pellets), I've been fed (muesli), and saddles are on. Packs still to be loaded. These camp routines make me so aware that no one can ever really bend to the rhythms of the desert, as I'd love to, and pull off this journey. To maintain the discipline of the march I'm forced to take account of days and hours. Though I don't wear a watch I'm aware of the sun's progress every moment. I wake when it's still dark, helped by a little alarm clock. Then I put the clock away for the day, mix the milk powder for my muesli and crank the camels into action, aware of the sun's advance right through until nightfall comes again.

*Later:* slowed down my walking pace as the sun rose and began burning off the mist, then the dew, then the moisture within the leaves. For a brief while sheltered under a tree in the bed of the Messum River. The camels became difficult. Nelson didn't like the look of The Brandberg – the vast block of rock oppresses him. And there are many unfamiliar sights and smells here. He likes to stop at any new shrub, sniff it, consider if it's edible. But he also likes to get to know his surroundings – their possible threats and pleasures. This is not a fantasy of mine. He makes a note of the dung of cats, hares, anything that is less familiar.

I'm camping at a road track which I've sought out in order to make a last rendezvous with John and Adrian. Above me is The Brandberg – magical, an ancient soul. I've sat down to admire it, falling under its power as people have done for at least six or seven thousand years – ancient rock paintings are scattered around the mountain's protective, weather-fluted sides. As I write, a hare has dipped into the dry riverbed below the red massif, then out, and zigzagged away through the rocks.

*Later:* soon after writing the above, in the early dusk, I fell asleep. Woke to find the camels gone. Worst nightmare. Not a sign, and impossible to track them through gravels. I headed south, into the wind. Nelson has always thought, quite rightly, that Oranjemund lies that way. Found him striding decisively – no doubt in his mind where he was going – with the others tagging behind. He chooses his moments carefully, then strikes out for freedom with terrifying speed. Caught up with him only because he'd stopped to chew a branch – much of it was still sticking out of his mouth.

A car came in the night, thumping along through the stones. It could only be John and Adrian – I flagged them in with my torch. John has been asking around about how to cope with lion attacks on the camels at night. Feels I must keep the three together on a rope held to my wrist. If the camels are together, the lions won't attack so readily. 'They like to single out a victim.'

John and Adrian now gone. They will place a couple of depots to the north. But from now on I'll be alone. Some sadness at parting, but not too agonizing seeing the little van disappear into the dust. It's been a gradual weaning process. I've now brought myself to a state of near total self-sufficiency.

### 28 October

Managed only 20 kilometres, even walking until dusk. My route veered up and around Table Mountain, through rocky spreads studded with welwitschia. Not one blemish yet on the camels' feet, but I'm now coming upon vertical strata beds of mica schists, ancient buckled-up sea muds. The land has been squeezed, tossed and clumsily relaid, the layers like a thousand mishandled pancakes. There is a sense of drama: such large forces at play, so many rock slices cutting out of the ground. Tomorrow I'll be heading through them.

*Twilight:* I only just had time to choose a camping sight where there was a boulder – the one which is meant to shield my head and encourage lions to go for my legs instead. To be attacked here would be unlucky as well as unfortunate – lions favour riverbeds, and though there was a sighting three weeks ago in the bed of the Ugab, that's still 15 kilometres away. Only on reaching there, tomorrow, will I have to (I'm told) get out my revolver.

THE MISTS OF BRANDBERG     139

# 8

# 'BETTER TO RISK THE SNAKES'

**29 October**
***Early morning:*** now into Damaraland, 'game country' – it'll soon be time to ponder whether to light fires to keep lions away, or douse them with water to stop rhinos charging through. Of course it hasn't escaped my notice that you don't, as a whole, get firewood in a desert.

Garth Owen-Smith, another authority out here, said I should 'watch out' for lions from about this point onwards. There are perhaps forty to fifty. Garth, who is based in Damaraland at a place called Wereldsend ('World's End'), woke one night in his sleeping bag to find he was about to be dragged off by a lion, which had him by the ankle. He fired his gun in the air, and the lion bounded off. Perversely, I'm sure the main threat to my success is just the humble stone.

***Later:*** there were soon rocks underfoot, and by the time the sun was high we were surrounded by them. Though these were old formations, the ground gave the impression it was still writhing and wrenching, prising open weaknesses in the strata and forming narrow valleys. We headed along an old track to the Ugab riverbed, from which the Save the Rhino Trust operated anti-poaching patrols.

Nelson became hesitant, unhappy to be led into what seemed to be a trap. Brown slabs encased us, magnifying the sound of our feet on the loose shale.

Then, added to this, came the sound of a far-off Land Rover. The vehicle

*Approaching the Obob River. The key to Nelson's continued co-operation was persuading him that his chances of survival were now somehow linked to mine. Meanwhile, Jan is tugging on the lead, the strain of the journey beginning to show.*

appeared, working slowly towards me. It was Blythe Loutit, from the Save the Rhino Trust. I'd met her before on a recce, and now remembered those soft, sensitive eyes of hers. She went up to say hello to the camels, and I wasn't surprised when they took an instant liking to her. She told me cheerily that she'd been searching for us for ages. She'd come to warn me about some of the rhinos.

'Warn me?'

'Just one or two of them.'

I began to hear about Mad Max, a rhino recognizable by his straight horns and habit of charging at absolutely anything. Apparently I was about to enter his home territory. There was also David, but he was 'more reasonable'.

I thought I might benefit from learning a little more. We headed down the track towards the Save the Rhino base camp, on the way passing the Brandberg West tin mine. Abandoned now, it looked like an organized junk yard. The men had been mining for tin, yet they'd had little houses made partly out of it – these were built entirely from car bumpers, exhaust pipes, radiators, oil drums.

I'm now at the base camp in the Ugab riverbed, valley walls pitching up to the sky, acacias spreading their branches, digging roots into subterranean waters.

Presently I'm sitting in the shade with the trackers, hearing all about Mad Max. Mateus, the camp boss, was almost got by him when he went for a spot of fishing. He had inadvertently chosen the same patch of river bank as the rhino, who was trying to have a snooze. The chase was on. Mateus 'ran up a cliff'.

Alfeus has also been chased, on this occasion at night, when Max ran through the patrol camp. The men attribute to him a magnificent cunning – tales of him waiting in ambush, of trackers tracked. Yet this animal is dependent on them for his very existence. There's been a 96 per cent decline in rhinos since 1970 – now there are about 110 left here. Part of the trouble is that rhinos are solitary, defending home ranges of over 100 square kilometres, and this makes it costly to defend them from poachers. But Save the Rhino are fighting back, with the help of their supporters – I'm writing while leaning against a Jeep donated by the artist David Shepherd. Mad Max, for one, certainly still seems to be alive and kicking.

It has been agreed that the anti-poaching unit, which is setting out on a ten-day patrol tomorrow, will go ahead of me. It's hoped they'll bump into Max first.

### 30 October

Walked on north through the canyons, loose rocks around us like fallen roof tiles, others jabbing into the sky. I began to see why Save the Rhino had been so concerned for me. There was nowhere to run. And even if I managed to 'run up a cliff' to escape, Nelson, Jan and Andries wouldn't be able to. As it was, the camels were nervous, unused to the overbearing rocks, the strange echoes. A slab would break away, apparently of its own volition, and scuttle down the slope, shifting more rocks as it came. But above all it was the threat of 1½-tonne Mad Max – bad-tempered, blinder than a bat – which bothered us. I say 'us' because the camels have developed an extraordinary ability to sense my mood. They know when I'm relaxed, and when I'm tense and alert. At present, I was tense and alert.

The sun lifted above the canyon and we were still walking, waiting for that ambush – the oncoming clomp of heavy feet. But it never came. The valley opened into a plain. Grasses, stiff and dry, spread to the distance. I could see around me for miles, and I realized it was only man, not rhino, that I didn't want to meet. For as far as the horizon, and probably way beyond, the world was undisturbed by humans, the likes of my own destructive kind.

In the midday stillness, the clink of a loosened rock plate – a Cape hare taking fright. Overhead, diminutive Gray's larks twittering. Gemsbok, young bachelors, stood watching us from a crest. After gazing some time, they too turned tail and fled, side-stepping, dodging, as if I was giving chase. Yet I was almost as vulnerable out here as they were. I still hadn't got out my revolver – when it had come to unpacking it yesterday, wearing a side-arm had seemed a touch melodramatic.

I've now stopped a moment, catching a scrap of shade in a tattered bush. The black stones absorb heat, and whenever I pause to check my heading with the compass the camels have to lift their feet in turn to cool them. We are away from the moderating influence of the sea. Summer is also approaching, and what's more every three days' walk I'm one degree nearer the equator.

I'll now turn west, heading towards what I hope will be Gai-As Spring. Don't need water, but, like a nervous car driver who calls in at a garage whenever the petrol gauge shows below half full, I feel better after a top-up. I'm never sure when the next supply will be. The next spring may be poisoned by a carcass.

*Later:* as we went on, more and more game trails were visible around me, coming in from barren hills, gullies. Lines made by the feet of zebra, gemsbok, springbok, kudu, radiating like the spokes of a wheel from a point ahead of me somewhere. There was no longer any doubt in my mind. I was almost at the spring.

I came at last to a pool among peat and reed clumps in the middle of a plain of shingle and rock. Up on the slope above, stone circles left from prehistoric times. Some rocks stacked very high still, like partial igloos.

*Twilight:* the sunset is vast, easily filling these wide horizons with an odd green light. As I look higher, this algal hue dims to a bluey copper sulphate, which in turn dissipates among the stars.

### 31 October

Travelled 22 kilometres onward to the Huab River. Before I left, took the camels to the spring and waited as Nelson drank his 70 litres – while on a march, camels instinctively know to fill their bellies while they can. Also here, Namaqua sandgrouse which had come from miles around. I became so entranced by the mass of life – these grain-feeders coming for their ritual dawn drink – that I forgot about the camels, who quickly departed. Not an escape bid, because the camels are coming to realize that my fate is somehow caught up with theirs, that they cannot afford to abandon me. Nelson was hoping just to elude me long enough to have a decent feast on the three or four thorn trees here.

In my haste to round the camels up, I almost trod on a snake. It was apricot brown and stretched out straight, warming itself. A shock, though the snake wasn't poisonous – it shot away rapidly and was probably only a Namib sand snake, where defence is speed and not bite. But I was suddenly reminded how vulnerable I am out here. I need only have one little accident, just once let my map fly out of my breast pocket … But staying alert all the time is so very hard.

As we walked on north, I thought about snakes again. Really only two I have to worry about: the puff adder which strikes at 6 metres per second and is, I think, the quickest of all strikers. Possibly there's also the zebra snake, or western barred spitting cobra, which doesn't need to be near water – it absorbs it instead from its prey. The bite delivers a complex and fatal mix of both cytotoxins and neurotoxins. Don't want to tread on too many of those before breakfast.

I was aiming for the Huab River, where André and Bertus Schoeman had one of their remote Fly-In Safari camps. Using my compass to set a course, I headed to a notched tooth of a peak, which should lie just behind their camp. The stones were now so densely spaced to make progress at all I had to stick to game tracks.

The sun beamed down heavily. Startled Namaqua sandgrouse rose from the thin grasses, clapping off in a squadron. They left a chick, silent and camouflaged among the freckled quartz, black dolomite and brick-red dust. The species nests

on the ground, and evades predators by way of this cryptic colouring but also by positioning itself away from the water sources which are the focus of other animals. Water is instead brought to the chick – the male sandgrouse, which has especially absorbent breast feathers, dunks himself in a spring then flies to the waiting offspring, which gathers the beads of moisture off him. Another tactic of life forms here is simply to store water, as the succulents do: I'd hoped to see some *Lithops ruschiorum* [Bushman's buttocks], stone-like buds in the gritty soil, but here on the plain there was only 'wolfsmilch' [wolves' milk] – an extremely spiny, thick-stemmed succulent that's something like a North American cactus.

The stones grew larger around our feet. Most had a black sheen, 'desert varnish', formed by dew evaporating and drawing out a thin deposit of silica. Other stones were heavy with iron, and where this had been oxidized they were the rusted red that is the source of the Himba ochre. As we walked by, the lack of living movement out here made me all the more aware of these insentient processes at work around us – great pleasure, a feeling of peace, from the silent ticking of the natural order of things. Our worries – our life and death – so insignificant. Yet here is a paradox: among all these processes, maybe all the processes in the universe, man is perhaps the only thing with the power to wonder. This makes us very significant.

In mid-afternoon we came to a halt. I found we were on a terrace, perched above the Huab Valley floor. Ahead, a panorama of hills made of brown sandstone – sands laid down by winds of the early Jurassic 200 million years ago. Also plateaux, blocks which had been protected by caps of ancient lava flows. Nelson took one look at the drop down, and wouldn't budge.

I worked back, then west along the terrace, a dolerite pipe, and was confronted by a small herd of Burchell's, or plains, zebra. Odd to see zebra among rocks – and these not even Hartmann's mountain zebra. A male stood in front, staring at the camels, daring them. In the heat haze he was magnificent and decorative, a knight's charger. Behind, six other zebras trotted from side to side, skittish but defiant. Then turned, leaving nothing but a beige cloud of dust.

And still that problem of getting down the terrace … I battled down the first, minor slope, aware that I might never be able to get the camels up again. Red boulders were still thick on the ground, the camels' feet rarely horizontal, and I was now hurrying – the sun was getting low. We paused for breath only once, by an elephant-foot plant, a stubby, silver specimen, the bulk of which is a globular base, its moist, potato-like flesh favoured by porcupines.

As the light began to soften we picked our way to a gentler incline, finally descending into a ravine. We were between vertical stone walls, hexagonal columns of basalt, other rocks in thick sheaths, books of them tumbling down as if from ransacked library shelves. When the ravine opened up, it revealed the *Phragmites australis* reed beds of the Huab – swifts skimmed the pools, mountain and familiar chats darted enthusiastically and a green and yellow bird, the bokmakierie, busied itself in dust patterned by the warped gnome feet of baboons.

So much life so suddenly – but no sooner had I stopped to enjoy it than I realized something was disturbing the camels – Nelson was stamping his feet, the others hunched up, sheltering against him. I led the camels on, and saw they were being attacked by horseflies. Jan, at the back behind Andries, was in a particularly bad way. It wasn't long before I saw that look in his eye – the one that means blind anger. If Jan bolted he would take the others with him – and my food and water. But I couldn't stop to undo the rein that tied him to Andries. So I walked the camels on, firmly addressing Nelson and at the same time trying to reach with my throwing knife to cut Nelson's line to Andries. This would lose me Andries and Jan, but if I could only control and keep Nelson they wouldn't go far.

Time was up. Jan began to trot, to kick at the air. Soon his baggage was loose and frightening him further. He took off, yanking Andries and Nelson along behind him. I ran with them, managing to get to Andries' rein and cut it, separating Nelson. It did little good. Off they went, in one mad bunch. Next moment I was standing alone in the ravine.

It was dusk. I had nothing, not even warm clothing. Nights aren't damp here, away from the coast, but the night temperature plummets. I took a deep breath and started running, following the camel prints. Came across a trail of my possessions – sleeping bag, soap, film, notebooks, Jan's saddle. When I did catch up with Jan and Andries, ten minutes later, it was only because Andries' foot had become entangled in his saddle, which he'd also tried to chuck. He was mooing for help, calling for me with that pleading look in his eye. I ran up, reassuring him, and finally cut him loose. I heaped all the things together and made Nelson carry most of it. I was furious with him. While I'd been untangling Andries he'd stood in the far distance, calling the others, offering to lead them all the way back to Oranjemund.

In the last light, I led the camels to the Schoeman camp. The zebra were still watching us from a rise, wondering what bizarre thing we'd get up to next.

### 1 November, at Kuidas Camp, Huab River

Neither André nor Bertus here, but their camp workers, all Hereros, have been helping me water the camels. The men edge around them suspiciously and study them through the reeds. I spent the day repairing my boots, doing ham-fisted stitching to keep the heat-blistered, rock-torn soles on.

*Right:* At dusk in Damaraland, removing Andries'
saddle. Having to walk, load and unload the
camels alone every day, as well as being ready to
run after escaping camels, meant keeping
absolutely fit and guarding against the slightest
injury – even of a sprained wrist – for six weeks,
the entire second half of the journey.

*Above:* Not much more than a splash of water was
spare for washing, and this only to clean cuts and
abscesses that had emerged when scratches were
infected by camel grime and aggravated by windblown sand. But this exposure to the terrain – no
luxuries, no radio communications, no backup
vehicle – was exhilarating, and, for me, the truest
expression of 'exploration' – letting go of our own
(Western) world in order to encounter another.

Behind the camp, above the spring, the chippings of Bushmen who sheltered here perhaps 5000 years ago. These people left etchings in the sandstones – the hoofprints of zebra, gemsbok and giraffe are repeated across the flat surfaces, as if on a hunter's scoreboard. And on one rock beside these prints, etchings of a human foot. The artist's signature? Or something less self-aware – a record of man's mark alongside those of other animals?

## *2 November*

It was a slow climb up from the Huab into hilly land behind – rusty rocks, sandstones enriched with pinkish feldspar. Angular boulders were strewn everywhere, and at the base of the valley a heap of stones which would have served to mark a Bushman grave, and of course protect the body from hyenas. Now travellers, when encountering these piles, traditionally add a stone of their own, thus ensuring – the tradition goes – that the spirit of the dead Bushman will walk with them as a guide. Unfortunately I was distracted with a mini-camel crisis as I walked past, and by the time I remembered it was a long way back. I pressed on, yet not having participated in this archaic ritual seemed to matter somehow.

Later I found myself thinking back to the graves of the diamond miners in the south – eye sockets filling with sand … The desert had been no more respectful of the white man's most precious ritual, for death, than for his strange quest for diamonds. The bones had been reduced to the status of the rest of the camp remains – no more than broken porcelain. But that's perhaps as it should be. Here in the desert you find yourself having to confront life and death, and all your fears and desires begin to appear as nothing compared to the grand forces at work. You feel privileged to have shared a part in the process at all. And I think it's that sense of privilege which lies behind the strength I've found, somewhat unexpectedly, in this seemingly pitiless environment. Whatever the root cause, I've a feeling that the Bushmen, with their everlasting spirits, their graves gathered from the rocks around them, understood all this more than we do.

Now I was heading into the Springbokwater Valley, home of lions if ever there was one. André Schoeman thought I'd probably be all right. 'When the lions see your camels – which they will – they'll probably just watch. They'd prefer to attack an animal they know.' He told a story about a lion that was seen at a spring drinking happily alongside a donkey. The donkey had never known a lion, and the lion had never known a donkey. They even sniffed each other, curious as to what they both were. The only discouraging part of André's story was that the donkey suddenly got a fright and trotted off – and immediately the lion pounced on it, breaking its neck. Animals often only attack when they sense fear. And by extension they – camels and lions alike – co-operate with the fearless.

Ostriches ran through the stones, springbok scattered, butterflies in white clouds knitted through the heat. Every animal we saw had the ability to move through here with ease. But we were at the mercy of the boulders, stumbling about as best we could. By late afternoon I was on a flat upland plain, starting to think about making a camp. But where? According to the leading experts, I was meant to sleep with boulders shielding my head from lions and with a slope at hand for evading rhino. There were never the two at the same time – and certainly no firewood. André had said that even a bush was better protection for your head than nothing. 'Better to risk the snakes.' But here there weren't even bushes. I kept walking until last light, knowing that the moon was almost full and would extend the day. Finally I homed in on one lone kokerboom [quiver tree], cramped between rocks, and battled to make the camels sit among all this rubble.

Now I am lying at the base of the tree. The tubular trunk and branches are extremely sparing in length, with little clusters of leaves on the stubby tips. Feel utterly drained – so tired I hardly care about the lions. I do have André's revolver ready, and have barricaded myself around with the saddles. I note that someone before me has singled out the same spot to shelter in, and made defences with stones. Meanwhile, the camels aren't the slightest perturbed. Their innocence is astounding. I have hobbled them all tightly. Better they stay put here, if a lion comes, and that I try to scare it off with a few rounds. I'm keeping the revolver loaded, placing it by my side with the first chamber empty. I'm so tired that I can't trust myself to think straight if I wake in the night with a fright. I need to be stopped from firing that first round in panic.

### 3 November

No lions. Rather a disappointment, after all that. On, down the Springbokwater River. At first I walked cautiously. I jumped each time springbok let out their startled alarm bark. Then I decided that the camels, with their height and good eyes, were, for all their innocence, my best look-out scouts. I peered whenever they peered. I looked back when they looked back. That lion … where was it?

No fresh lion spoor by midday, but some of rhino. Sometimes a branch that a rhino had recently chewed and discarded. And now the warm air on my face was lulling me. The hours after noon are the most dangerous part of the day on the African plain. All is quiet, the springbok and gemsbok sleepy as the cats move in … I felt the dulling of my senses too as the heat rose off the ground, the air fizzed slowly with the riverbed crickets. I was growing careless, and knew it, and hardly cared. Only the tug of Nelson's rein, when he yanked at a clump of grass, kept me

*View south towards the Huab River, from Kuidas Camp, Terrace Springs. This spring was visited by Bushmen, and later by semi-nomadic herders who left rings of stones which probably once supported the poles of their shelters. However, as the Namib has become increasingly arid, the herds of zebra (*Equus zebra*), giraffe (*Giraffa camelopardalis*) and gemsbok (*Oryx gazella*), whose prints the Bushmen have engraved in the rocks above the spring, have depleted and the people who relied on them forced to retreat.*

from falling asleep on my feet. Eventually I succumbed, and allowed myself forty winks propped with my back shielded by a tree.

*Twilight:* just now, I met a herd of gemsbok – beautiful, with their slow, swinging, black sweeping tail as they canter. This remarkable animal can survive for hours with body temperatures of 45 degrees C – 42 degrees is lethal to most animals. The trick lies in the gemsbok keeping its brain temperature down. It pants heavily, cooling special nasal blood vessels which lead off around the skull.

I've moved out of the riverbed – lion land – and have parked the camels on a terrace slope. Now all three camels have their heads flat on the ground in total exhaustion. Sometimes their eyes wander over to me, hopefully, but I have nothing for them – no water, no food. As usual, I've built up the saddles to protect my head when I sleep – one behind, one to either side. Wasn't it out here that some-

*Despite the popular image of camels as desert dwellers, they need large quantities of water to survive arid conditions. Before setting out, Nelson would drink up to 80 litres, and this sustained him for a week. Gemsbok (*Oryx gazella*), on the other hand, can survive without water, obtaining sufficient moisture from grazing. Not having a camel's strong herd instinct, they are able to wander alone in search of grazing.*

one had his nose bitten off by a spotted hyena? They're far more aggressive than the strandwolf, or brown hyena, of the coast, but both species can easily crack open a tin can – not that they've yet shown any interest in the meatballs.

Nelson sits by me like a spoilt pet dog, waiting for titbits. Gives a nip to the others if they try to get in the front of the queue.

### 5 November
Today passed through Springbokwater Gate, through the quarantine fence which keeps foot-and-mouth and other cattle diseases from southern Africa. It runs magnificently right across the country, except where the elephants have flattened it.

A hazy, cool day. Stone fields, and gravel plains that are so flat between the red plateaux that they look steam-rollered. The last two nights I haven't slept, disturbed not by lions but by mosquitoes. Feel drained in the day, impatient with the poor camels and they don't know why. Decided to ride a while on Nelson – the first time since the start of the journey. Still the same conservative, slow chap. Still swings his tail from side to side, like a contented old dog, when he urinates.

**Night-time:** a full moon, fleece clouds. The camels silhouetted. They sit, looking about dreamily. Do they never sleep?

### 6 November, Uniab River

Cloudy, at times overcast. Plateaux of dull mud browns, plains coloured by rich ochre, conjuring visions of Himba stepping from the landscape and encouraging me on. The Himba lands are not far away now … Rode Nelson again. He resents it more today – doesn't want this to become a habit.

We came to the Uniab river – swaying shrubs and the thickest vegetation I have yet seen. Much rhino dung – they've been eating rough grass and a thistly type of plant that Nelson also now craves.

As we came down into the riverbed, another attack by biting flies. I separated the lead reins, quickly drew the camels to a brackish spring, let them slake their thirst and tried to hurry them away. But too slow. The flies bit and Andries suddenly ran amok, wiggling out of his saddle. This set off Jan, who did the same. I soon had the situation contained but both camels were again lucky to jettison a saddle with its full load without damaging their limbs. I can't let this happen again. This time, they broke only two girth straps.

### 7 November

Harassed, when the dawn came up, by gnats. A battle to get the camels saddled up. They were scraping their heads through bushes as the gnats tried to drink from their eyes. Biting flies joined in the torment as the sun rose, and the camels now used their muscular tails as whips.

After we had got away I stopped only once, suddenly finding myself staring at the ground. No mistaking it. A lion's spoor, the paws about as large as my hands. The tracks looked fresh, each pad crisp and clear in the ochre dust, there was no way of telling exactly how old they were – maybe an hour, maybe a month. The desert gravels can preserve the marks of vehicles for centuries. However, I followed the track back down into the riverbed dust and found that the lion had disturbed the dew there. It had been through only this morning. The lion was heading east, upriver – which suited me, because I was heading north.

I was now heading for the Obob River, which would lead me, I hoped, to a spring near its headwaters. At 5 p.m., as I was still making my way over a smooth rise, thinking about making camp, a small plane flew over. It was weaving back and forward, obviously trying to find me. This must be John and Adrian. They couldn't spot me – so much for any search-and-rescue operation – and so I spread the camels out against the darker rocks. The light was fading: when I might have been preparing camp, and making that much-talked-about fire for fending off lions, I had to stand around waving, using the camels as a signpost. While I waved in vain, I noticed elephant dung everywhere around me. The only obvious shelter from wildlife was a bush that had been half rubbed away, bludgeoned by the buttocks of elephants wanting a good scratch.

On what must have been the plane's last sweep – it was virtually dark – they dropped me a message from the sky. I opened the container.

A letter gave instructions for finding Armspoort, a point on the Hoanib River, a few days from here. Mike Hearn, from Save the Rhino, would arrange for a patrol to drop off a drum of water, and also food supplies for ten days. The food would be in a tin box to protect it against baboons. 'You are now entering an area extremely rich in game,' the note went on, 'elephant, rhino and LIONS, lots of them – and that's a fact. Be careful – I am being serious. John.'

Due to having waited for the plane it was too late now to go grubbing around for firewood, so I settled the camels down, just out of the riverbed, and built up a protective wall of saddles. I poured some paraffin into my little lamp and lit it up. And here I am. Again, the camels are double hobbled, so they can't shift. I've got my revolver ready – placed it under a cloth, but in easy reach.

### 8 November

***Early morning:*** it was a surprisingly short time before the lions began to make their presence known last night. But not the roar that you get in Hollywood. The Namib lions tend to be quiet – they are under-populated and don't need to advertise their huge territories. So I lay there hearing nasal grunting, not roaring.

There were two lions, perhaps three. Behind, to the south, spread out a little. The distance was hard to judge – 200, maybe 300 metres away to our west. They were getting nearer. Or perhaps just clearer, with the breeze dropping, the grass no longer shifting. I picked up the gun, clicked the chamber forward one. Grunt, grunt from those lions. They were prowling, investigating, deciding …

The camels were totally unconcerned. Munch, munch, munch. I could see their heads in the moonlight. I watched them – it was calming, even though the camels were behaving with a naiveté bordering on utter stupidity. Some time in the night I dropped off to sleep, unable to wait for the lions any longer. I woke once or twice, for some reason checked that the revolver was still there, and slept again. At last came the first haze of dawn light, and I felt safe.

# 9

# LATE-NIGHT GUESTS

**8 November**

***Evening:*** over low red rolling hills, springbok and ostrich scattering. They are alarmed, I think, not by the unfamiliar profile of the camel – its hefty body perched so high in all this sparseness – but by the baggage on them, the alien black and red colours, the muffled clanking of mug against plate. We dropped into the Obob River, meandering between impressive cliffs and just as impressive, though not fresh, lion tracks.

A white-faced scops owl blinked in a rock crevice. Towards the head of the river the air was thick with the musky, pungent smell of the 'mustard bush'. I began looking out for Crowthersquelle Spring, a freshwater source which was said to harbour a thicket of trees. No sign, so we climbed out of the riverbed and looked down from the high cliffs. Not far off was an oasis, jade green leaves shivering in the wind. Small birds twittered in busy flocks – always a sure sign of water. While I was still looking, Nelson tugged his lead rein out of my hands and began walking off with fixed intent. I was annoyed, thinking he was heading for one of his thistle things. Then I became scared. He was aiming for the cliff edge and I suddenly knew he must be able to smell water. I'd already seen how the camels become entranced by that smell, become gripped by powerful desert animal instincts. If this had been Andries or Jan – now walking fast up behind Nelson – they would have been over the cliff by now. Nelson, though, stopped at the brink.

*Giraffes (Giraffa camelopardalis), known for their inquisitiveness, at times seemed besotted with the camels and often followed them. Being able to spend silent days alone with elephant (Loxodonta africana) and giraffe was perhaps the greatest privilege of the journey.*

He just stood there, savouring the damp smell in the breeze. I led the camels safely down to the riverbed, and Nelson took me to the water.

## 9 November

Sad, resigned look on Nelson's face as we were leaving the vegetation of Crowthersquelle.

## 10 November

**Before departure:** that's all I managed to write for yesterday. So tired every night. No last reflections on the day, no tossing or turning, just a dead sleep. I do open an eye sometimes, woken by camel snufflings and possible lion surveillance, and more camel snufflings.

Camped in a minor river course. Small birds – one trills, another chirrups. The odd gemsbok, standing to attention on distant pink outlying hills, as I get on with the job of chewing through my meatballs. As a rule, I don't cook them – it brings out the flavour.

Next to me, a giant *Euphorbia damarana*, a plant composed of poisonous silver-green strands which ascend like plastic rods to the sky. In an empty valley of thin grasses, the plant was an easy choice for sleeping place – no lion was going to get through 3 metres' worth of *that*. It's the only vegetation that seems actually to enjoy life out here – it's untroubled by even desperate grazers, being armed with a toxic milky sap. It sits not like a plant, but like a clutch of crystalline strands.

Moon waning and coming late in night, lighting the camp for my 5.30 a.m. rise. Then my muesli and one and a half hours of packing before I set foot anywhere. A jackal this morning, calling across the plain. A lonely cry, suggesting utter dejection and abandonment.

I'm not lonely out here. The desert draws you to it: not like oppressive jungle, which squeezes in on you with its competitive life forms, each telling you you're the odd one out. Here, even a snake seems like a friend. You are allies, in this together.

**Afternoon:** following game trails, at midday reached the water hole known as 'Hunkab'. I approached the water with caution. I now see these springs not as fountains of life, but as places of great danger. The camels forget any loyalty to me – they have thoughts only of water. As we came near I kept my voice up, reminding them they were being monitored. 'Jan, I'm watching you. Slowly. Slowly, Nelson … *Jan*!' This does control them if they haven't already wound themselves up into a state. Even so, today I had to wrench at Nelson's halter to get his attention. Once he was at the water's edge, he ploughed his head into the water. He kept walking deeper to avoid the dirt clouds his feet made. The water was fairly saline, and caused the camels to toss their heads to get the taste from their mouths. While they barged about, a falcon swooped along the gully and clouds of smaller birds lifted, turned and mobbed the bird of prey until it retreated.

My intention had been to fill up my own water supply at the springhead, where the water was less saline, but then the horseflies moved in. I scrambled with the camels up the hill slopes, over rocks, getting them into the breeze and away. I have 17 litres left for myself. Should be ample until my depot on the Hoanib River, about two days away.

Over more rocky plains, these the territory of Van Gogh, a rhino with one ear. Not a troublesome rhino, people say, but I see that he's squashed rather a lot of bushes. Some of these are the poisonous *Euphorbia damarana*, and I wonder if this behaviour is to smear its alkaloids on his skin to remove skin parasites.

Lots of the 'thistle' that the rhinos – and Nelson – are forever seeking. I let Jan loose to follow us, so he could get maximum grazing and put on some weight. Later he actually overtook us – unheard of, for this professional lagger. Then he parked himself down in our path. It couldn't have been a clearer request to me to halt. Yet his pack is small – only my water, emergency food tins and my clothes – about 40 kilos total.

***11 November***

***8.30 a.m.:*** slept against a rock buttress composed of layer upon layer of ancient sediment. This region, the Hunkab River and the area to the north-east, is one of the big lion areas – yet not a peep from any here, so far. I was warned they might 'walk along' with me out of curiosity. (In itself enough to make the camels run, with fatal consequences.) But nothing. I'm getting less cautious at night – though I keep my revolver by my 'pillow', which is my folded jumper. When the moon rose, the camels broke some of their hobbles, and hopped off to graze. Rounded them up in my bare feet – and this morning saw a baboon spider amble right through my camp. It had a tarantula's body bulk, and fangs as black and shiny as deadly nightshade. I remember an Afrikaner child calling this the 'thigh tickler'.

The camels now have an acute awareness of what I expect of them. They look repentant, after they've been gallivanting; and they behave like one-humped angels when there's food around or when they need comfort.

Rocks, rocks. Gneiss, red from feldspar, running north–south. I can expect this formation to continue, on and off, right to the Hartmann Valley.

*Their* feet are still lasting. My boots, however, have given up the ghost. I'm now on to my eighth pair– no ankle support. I'll bind my ankles when this becomes necessary.

**Below:** *Far from enjoying the sight of fresh water, I began to fear it. The camels, driven by powerful survival instincts, became like over-excited children, and would frolic in cool water and mud.*

**Right:** *A second later, biting flies would suddenly attack, sending the camels into panic. Here, Adrian, the photographer, was on hand to record the incident, but when I was alone it was more than a little unnerving to see them disappearing with all my food, shelter and water. In effect, flies were a greater hazard than any lion.*

***Later:*** so much grass, so few grazers. It's a sign of how unusually heavy the rains were this year – the small herds of springbok hardly dent the food supply.

In the morning I came to a picturesque *Euphorbia damarana* and talked to my video camera about its dangers. I quoted Mike Hearn's story of about thirteen dim men – Ovambos, I think – who came down from the north, looking for work, and cooked up their meat on a fire made from its roots. Later their bodies were found neatly side by side as they'd slept. As I told the story to the camera (I'm on number 5 already) I looked over my shoulder to see Jan plucking a euphorbia pod. I punched him in the stomach and the pod came flying out. He began shaking his head – just the bitter taste, I hoped. I undid his rein to let him walk free, in case he suddenly went berserk. Rhinos and kudu seem to have become partly adapted to the alkaloids, and eat the pods, but if Jan had consumed one I didn't fancy his chances. I kept an eye on him all day. However, though he didn't eat and was particularly aloof all day, he was back to his strange self by nightfall.

Down the Mudorib, a rocky gully tributary of the Hoanib. Walls of rock, trees bursting from them. Like a Japanese garden, conjunctions of opposite forms, the non-breathing and the breathing. Stark grey striated rock, rising abruptly, trees such as camel thorn delicate in the riverbed. A vulture's nest heaped in one tree, threatening to topple it. Scuttlings in overhead rocks – chacma baboons following us, perhaps. It seemed a private place. Springbok stared, reluctant to move on. But my eyes were ahead. This was elephant country. Bedsheet-size strips of bark torn away. Dung scattered in football-size clumps; birds foraging in it.

At dusk, as I made camp, I heard a clatter in the riverbed gravels. A lone giraffe loped into view. It caught sight of the camels and stopped, transfixed. The camels gazed back. For a while they were locked together, studying each other, like people wondering if they've met before somewhere. Eventually the camels lost interest – they wanted to get on with their end-of-day grazing. But the giraffe lingered. When I approached, it did canter off – that slow-motion leg swing. But it turned and followed me as I walked back to the camp. Southern giraffes, like all giraffes, are naturally inquisitive, but it was as if he was lonely and had mistaken the camels for his own kind. Young male giraffes such as these don't form bachelor groups but move singly between herds; when they do mate, they tend to leave the females to bring up the young. As I walked back I noticed how closely, in the dusk, the giraffe and camels resembled each other – the height, the long neck, the dark eyebrows, the dark tail. I remembered that the Afrikaans word for giraffe is kameelperd, 'camelhorse'.

Lit a fire for the first time – firewood at last. Too tired to enjoy it.

## 12 November

To the depot. Easy to find: before Armspoort, at the confluence of the Mudorie and Hoanib. The food, as Save the Rhino promised, in a baboon-proof tin. Took out the supplies, and replaced them with my litter, and also my boot remains. Not amused to discover that I've been provided with more meatballs.

Camels fought over the water in the drum. While Andries was having his turn, Jan stuck his head between my legs and upset the bowl: 20 litres was spilt, and all three camels rammed their heads into the ground, chasing the water beads as they sped away across the hard earth.

I thought I'd spend a day or so in the riverbed: thick, scented air, mature acacias arching overhead. It was as if we were lodged in savannah – exquisite shady bowers, softness after so much hard rock. No open water here, but here and there you could see where animals had dug into the riverbed for it, scooping dust to the side. Chacma baboons up on the cliff side stared at me as they scratched themselves. They had guards which sat comfortably on peaks, barking warnings. As we came by the troops moved off, mothers ambling away up the scree, some with babies slung around them.

The nutritious pods of the ana tree, favourite morsel of the elephants, were now ripe, and sometimes they dropped down, rattling through the tree crowns. There was dung scattered everywhere, and the elephants themselves wouldn't be far away. They walk east to Dubis Spring, fill up with water, then wander back down the riverbed, collecting the crimson ana tree pods as they go. Eventually they arrive at the coastal dunes, where there is trapped water, and refill before launching once more upriver.

## 13 November

Slept on a terrace among grass and devil's thorn, a yellow-flowered, spindly shrub armed with a multi-faceted thorny burr – perfect size to slip between sock and shoe. Slightly worrying sleeping so near the main river course in view of the large elephant population, but there wasn't any choice.

A night free of disturbance. In the morning headed on east, upriver. We followed an elephant trail, a smooth band of dust that was two-elephant-feet wide. The dung strewn along it was becoming more and more fresh. Nelson carefully sniffed each ball he came across – to such an extent that I had to plot a course avoiding them. I knew what was bothering him: gemsbok have dung the size of peas, giraffe dung is the size of large hazelnuts, so how big is an animal that leaves dung the dimensions of a soccer ball? Large birds were rummaging through them and apparently dining well.

*The Obob River. There were many lion spoor in the locality, and although
they must have been aware of us, we never saw them. With such large territories, the lions
(*Panthera leo*) of the Namib seldom roar to advertise themselves. I heard their grunts as they
edged towards my camp, probably curious about the camels.*

We proceeded slowly, passing tree barks scored by tusks. The parallel lines
seemed like graffiti – signatures and statements. From the look of the tracks we
were on the heels of an adult with wrinkly feet, a second elephant with feet only
wrinkly in parts, and a third one which was only a calf. Giraffe cantered away,
their heads a counter-lever to their rear legs. A family of ostriches stormed by – a
dozen tawny grey juveniles running in a tight fleet, their feet kicking up a high
dust cloud. Nelson began to get agitated, slightly frightened. I'd never seen him
quite like this – he'd been angry at times, flustered, restless, scared at the Lange
Wand waves, but this was terror. I stopped, held the lead rein tight and poked
some dung with my foot. The great cake fell open. This was absolutely fresh – it
released steam. Nelson reared away, but did follow me when I tugged.

The Namib elephants have taken on mythic status, and guidebooks talk of
them as specially adapted to the rigours of desert – thicker feet to stop bruising,

bigger ears to fan with. But the truth is that they are standard *Loxodonta africana*, separated by farms from their fellows which frequent the inland pans of Etosha. Depleted by poaching and by the drought of the early Eighties, they maintain themselves by plodding huge distances. When necessary they delve into the dust to create new water holes, and if the babies can't reach with their trunks, the aunts and mothers suck up the water themselves and squirt it into their mouths.

As we went on, Nelson scanned the trees ahead. The elephants would be down-wind of us, but maybe he was picking up the inaudible noises that elephants are now known to communicate with.

I had expected to be given lots of warning – a solid land mammal blocking the way ahead. Instead we were right in front of the first elephant before we saw it – I stopped only when I realized that the tree shadow ahead was filled entirely by something like a breathing boulder. It was incredible. How could such a mass be lost in the shade of a tree? Only the slow flap of its ears gave the elephant away, a steady rhythm like that of a fish's gills working. Nelson had had enough. He pulled violently on the lead, and I was dragged away. It was a most undignified evacuation. I glanced over my shoulder and saw the elephant watching placidly – the ears opening, closing, opening, closing …

A short distance away I managed to get the camels securely hobbled. As I left to go and look at the elephants, Nelson let out a short bellow of distress. He tried to walk away on his knees. I patted him – 'Back soon, I promise' – gave each of the camels a bunch of grass, took my camera tripod and went to find the elephants. They appeared rather before I was expecting them: six, coming towards me. Then all six disappeared, vanished into a clump of low salvadora. Again I stared in disbelief. How could a small herd of elephants vanish in front of my eyes? As I walked forward to follow them, a large trunk stuck out from another bush, to my left, and sniffed the air. The elephant, a young bull, was only 20 metres away, but wasn't agitated by my presence – he seemed to be too busy sniffing the scent coming from the camels.

Another elephant moved in from behind me, and I had to duck away between the bushes so as not to be trapped between them. I was alone out here – no safari vehicle, no guide – and it had struck me, and perhaps the elephants, that my tripod resembled a gun. Many relatives of these very individuals had been shot by poachers in front of their eyes. For all I knew they might also be angry about the incident with the Italian tour leader this year near Palmwag – he had chucked a stone at an elephant to get a better photo and, after giving repeated warnings, the elephant lost his temper. He actually hunted the Italian down, chasing him around a bush, trampling him to death and giving him a light toss, like salad.

My experience was considerably less fraught, as it turned out. I stayed with the two elephants for the rest of the day while they walked about plucking up the ana tree pods and, as the heat intensified, hung in the shadows, flapping those ventilating ears. They dozed, scattered cool dust on their backs, or lazily plucked another pod. Sometimes they clashed tusks. The elephants seemed to have accepted my presence and were simply getting on with their lives – only from time to time one or other elephant would raise his trunk to catch my scent.

When the sun began sinking I didn't want to leave: I was alone in the desert with creatures of such power. But they were slowly moving downriver, towards the trussed up camels. I slipped away to rescue them. Nelson was desperately looking around, trying to catch sight of me. I got the feeling he had been doing so for the whole five hours I'd been away.

I had some difficulty finding a suitable camp. It was a question of waiting to see which side of the narrow valley the two bull elephants would come, and they were veering whimsically back and forth. Finally I gave up waiting for them to decide, and manhandled the camels up on to a high, stony terrace. As I unsaddled the camels, another lone giraffe came to watch. Like the one before, it seemed obsessed by the idea of getting to know Nelson.

The elephants came at dusk. Nelson watched them go by, noting how they clutched grass, swiped pods from branches, picked them from the dust. After a short while, he again tried to crawl away to hide.

Now it's night, the camels are tied securely. The elephants are still down there. They mock-charge at each other, giving a grunt, then a trumpet blast. The sound echoes down the valley, a brassy vibration that hangs in otherwise tranquil air.

### 14 November

**Dawn:** the elephants finally left, trumpeting as they went – like that type of guest who merrily hoots his car horn as he waves goodbye. Two pied crows moved in and sat releasing a bubbly cackle. I miss these eccentric little characters when they aren't around to watch over me. Lightning last night in the eastern sky. Must be careful of flash floods. The waters come in a warning trickle, then a solid wall. Which river was it that swept away three giraffes this year? Branches, boulders, even other trees are still jammed against the upriver side of the acacia trunks here.

I walked west, back down the river, with a view to continuing north at Armspoort, where the river is squeezed by a tight gully. Unfortunately the two bull elephants hadn't progressed very far and it wasn't long before Nelson came to a grinding halt near one of them. At first he stood as if hypnotized. The elephant stood patiently swaying to left and right, watching with his expressionless little eyes. I managed to find an alternative route, dragging the camels through the salvadora bushes and eventually back to the main riverbed – only to find that the elephant had moved on and was now ahead of us again. For the next two hours we were zigzagging on the terraces, trying to overtake. This was like being stuck behind an annoying lorry on a country lane. The second bull appeared from behind, causing Nelson more traumas – and just when Nelson couldn't stand any more, three giraffes turned up to ogle at him.

Yesterday was Dad's birthday. I forgot. I have sunk completely into another world – scared of remembering the death of someone out there who cared for me. But it's a measure of how much resilience I've gathered from the desert – the robustness of the Himba, the eternity of the rocks – that this evening I now feel able to let some of that other world reach me. Memories come in sad pangs. Last year, for Dad's seventieth birthday, we were going to have a party. The plans never materialized. 'The main thing is for Mum to get better first.'

### 15 November

In a week or so I'll be in Kaokoland with the Himba, people I count as friends. Three months ago, when I met Kwazarane, I thought the girl might have to guide me through the stone fields. Now I think there's a very good chance that both the camels and I will weather them.

From just east of Armspoort, the river bottleneck, I turned north up the Tsuxub Valley, which I hoped would give me a clear route through to the Hoarusib, the next substantial river system. We were ascending a wide valley hemmed by age-old immovable rocks and floored with an exquisite lawn of grass. The blades were thinly scattered, but the effect of the lilac and lemon stems was to soften the landscape. The land appeared to sway as the grasses billowed in the wind, waves running up and down the hills. We moved quickly – Nelson still running from the elephants. Bees pestered Jan, trying to drink water from the neck of the container he was carrying. He began to prance as they buzzed his ears. I had to stop the camels, make them sit while the bees menaced, and give the container to the only camel with the slightest sense of responsibility, Nelson.

The valley opened towards its head. I stood looking out on the plains around, towards the rockscape horizons. In all this region I could see only one tree. A one-off species standing alone in a spread of a billion grass blades. Coming across the lone thorn tree was like coming across someone to talk to. It was a higher being, one that had determination, that said it was here to stay. However, being the valley's only tree brought with it heavy duties – it had been used as an elephant backscratcher, a gemsbok sunscreen, a giraffe lunch break. Birds by the thousand had perched on it, grateful for the rest. Guano was stacked high, like candlewax, on the branches. And now I too had sought out the thorn tree. I wanted it as a friend, and had brought along three camels to boot.

***Twilight:*** and light is playing on the outlying hills, illuminating them with yellow, immersing them in a soup of blue. Rain clouds are moving in, some of them the dark of angry seas. I can smell rain – I'm cursing, Andries jubilant. I'm about to make a tent by pitching layers of camel blankets over my BBC tripod.

The camels are very tired. I walked relentlessly today, giving them little time in which to graze, and now I have no horse pellets for them. Jan is lying on his side, his head stretched on to my sleeping bag, breathing into my lap. The 'Killer Camel' lying prone, virtually in my hands. Total acceptance of me – or is he too tired to care? He serves as a useful table: I've laid out my map on him. But I do worry about you, Jan old thing.

### 16 November

Awoke wet, but dried in the wind as I walked – the smoothly rounded hills lifting and sinking, a girder of sharper mountains around. Other hills also appeared right in front of us, rearing granites, whole ranges swelling up on either side of

*There is no evidence that the elephants (*Loxodonta africana*) of the Namib are 'desert-adapted', though it's often said. They are part of the inland population, now cut off by encroaching farms, and survive by trudging long distances between water holes, using their natural intelligence to overcome any obstacles in their way – and even seem to enjoy a slide down dunes on their backsides.*

the Hoarusib Valley as it ran east–west across our horizon. We descended a rocky gully, Nelson stopping time after time to examine elephant dung. I knew that we were nearly at the riverbed when he began overtaking me: water.

We were soon in the canyon bed, and I was fighting the camels as they frolicked on the reeds and rich green swathes. There wasn't much water, just a dribble, but it was fresh. They were dizzy with excitement. Andries sat down heavily in the stream mud. Seeing that he had got away with it, Jan and Nelson copied. I had to drag all three camels to the sand terrace, and there fought a pitched battle to hobble them and get the saddles and packs off. All three were soon back in the stream, rolling in the mud. They were still at it at sunset.

Porrus, the second of the Schoemans' Fly-In Safari camps and also my next depot, well within reach for tomorrow. Thank God – not because it's a potential rest, though Jan needs it – but because it's an important milestone. Many people didn't think I'd get this far. Now people will have to say, 'Well, the poor bloke did at least reach Porrus.'

## 17 November

I wrote the above just before rounding up the muddy camels and bringing them back to my camp for the night. I remember thinking that something was wrong. I knew these camels – I'd spent three months hearing every breath of theirs, day and night. But my feeling of disquiet wasn't strong, and I put it down to my usual unease at being near water. I shouldn't have let the camels play. This expedition wasn't a game – it's even conceivable that one day my life might depend on them being a disciplined team. And look at them now: a rabble covered head to toe in black mud.

However, by dark the camels had settled down. They began to chew the cud, Nelson grinding his teeth with an excruciating squeak as he sometimes does as if to annoy me. All was calm. I remember because of what happened next. The first thing I asked myself afterwards was: were the camels simply over-excited from playing in the river?

I wrote my diary, blew out my paraffin lamp, laid out my revolver. Dozed off. The next thing, I was wide awake. The camels in a state – hopping about, breaking hobbles, really frightened. I turned on my torch – always kept by the gun. The camels were hardly visible under the black sky. I picked up the revolver and stood up. Something was out there. Swung the torch beam along the riverbed, looking for the eyes of an animal. My first thought was: lions. The camels knew hyenas – they'd let them pad around the camp. They knew jackals, and had treated them just like eccentric dogs. Rhino? Possibly, but to find one here was pushing it a bit. Elephant – a real possibility. But I'd have heard an elephant myself. That left lions – but again, we were very much on the edge of their range. Except that no one really knows.

By now I was as tense as the camels. We had been standing there, all four of us, looking into the night. Not a good feeling – blackness all around. Listening was hard – with Jan's nasal breathing and Andries hopping and fidgeting. The stream as well made trickling, lapping noises, dirtying the night silence. I stepped over to Nelson, told him to 'koes.' He sat, reluctantly. The others followed suit.

I lay down, and finally fell asleep again. Next thing the camels were on their feet, careering about. Once more, there was no doubt in my mind that there was something out there. I asked myself, 'Am I overdramatizing?' I remembered when I had felt threatened by a small cat in the Amazon. People in England had laughed at the idea – the cat looked like, and probably was, a variety of the harmless ocelot – but in that case I was proved right by the local Indians [filmed giving an account of a man killed in broad daylight]. They'd abandoned the village of Remo-yacca and re-settled downriver, as a result of this unnaturally aggressive behaviour, which spooked them.

I made myself light my lamp – a way of slowing myself down. The camels at that moment began hopping away as best they could. I went into a drill. Quite calmly I fired two rounds into the air. The two blasts thudded on the narrow valley walls and bounced around. The darkness felt very silent after that.

I listened, and heard nothing. The camels were far off. I waited, listening. Nothing. Then to my annoyance I realized that I couldn't just leave the camels out there by themselves. I was going to have to get them. I walked off into the night, probing the dark with the torch and feeling watched by every lion, every hyena, every frog. My heart was thumping hard, the revolver no comfort at all. How was I going to do what Tommy Hall had advised – stick it in the lion's mouth? I couldn't even see my own feet in this blackness.

The camels had crossed the stream. I talked a little to them, re-tied their hobbles and waited, sitting down against Nelson. I felt much safer now, within his snug warmth. I didn't want to go back to my camp. However, after waiting quite a while, and with no disturbance, I set off back again and finally, went to sleep.

This morning I couldn't find any tracks – not surprising among pebbles. I moved off upriver quickly – there would be biting flies when the sun got up.

Soon, as at the other springs, the water that was so vital to us was also our greatest threat. For the first three hours I couldn't even stop to drink because the flies were pestering the camels so badly. Even Nelson tried to throw off his saddle. I longed for a sight of Porrus – a genuine oasis with shady palms, food supplies, even a radio on which to talk to Adrian.

At last the valley broke right open into level sands, thick tree groves and the odd makalani palm. Humans again, Herero women ogling at us while washing underwear by the river. They stared through the heat, then ran to spread the news. At long last the camels and I were out of the river and safe. It was a moment to savour. Or rather it should have been. But there was no view, no expanse to occupy. Instead, Herero villagers laughing and screaming with excitement. We were zoo animals suddenly. It was impossibly confining after the peace that we'd come to know – and now needed. The camels made a run for it. I was only just quick enough to get out of their way. Yes, we'd successfully made it to the oasis of Porrus, but we couldn't stand it. And the camels had carried on, into the liberty of the wastes beyond.

# 10

# HARTMANN
# AND THE HEAT

**20 November, into Kaokoland**

Departed Porrus. Happy to be on the road again. And it's not just me. The camels set off determinedly and were rather quiet, as if recovering after a shock. They wanted to keep moving – perhaps the energy pent up in their huge legs after a few days' rest, or perhaps, as I like to think, they've changed from farm-softened animals that fear the hardship of the desert to ones that have realized their camel potential and found a niche in it.

We walked rapidly, sticking to the extensive dry terraces of the Hoarusib. This is a wide, deep valley – hints of forces from a different epoch, certainly forces larger than today's water that is dribbling through the rocky schists. In fact the valley's expansive shape dates from the beginning of the Karoo sequence, 200–270 million years ago, when much of Namibia was covered in ice sheets. Difficult to imagine, through the heat haze, the valleys of the Hoarusib and Khumib being ground down by the glaciers moving through.

Rising excitement. First signs of the Himba. So far the herders themselves are absent, but the ground is trampled by their cows, the dust jabbed by the feet of a

*Spied by Adrian, who took this photograph as we neared the Himba settlement of Onyuva. While Nelson habitually kept his eyes ahead, I kept mine to the ground to negotiate a passage through the stones. I had been advised by many that a journey with camels through the rocks of Damaraland and the stony hills of Kaokoland would be near impossible. The expedition proved to the Save the Rhino Trust that they could use them successfully on anti-poaching patrols.*

hundred goats. We've passed through old settlements, the huts now skeletons, mud and dung falling away. When the rains happen to favour this valley, and the grasses are once more soft and green, the Himba will again drift in this direction, bringing with them their herds.

Of course I'm wondering where the family that I knew have wandered – Kwazarane, Wapenga (the uncle with the wheezy laugh) and his wife Ka-ada. The settlement in which I saw them, Omungunda, must be three or four days north of here in the heart of Kaokoland. If I make it there through the stones, I am really virtually clear. I'll be on the home straight, up the Hartmann Valley to the Kunene River. Or isn't it as simple as that?

Nelson's favourite plant, the 'thistle', belonged to gravel plains and is long since behind us. Now he's found another, a pretty tree parasite – clearly a mistletoe with red, blushing leaves. Nelson has now learnt to spot it at fifty paces.

### 21 November, Otjovaurwa settlement

In the morning, walked through another Himba village. This one was occupied – many of the huts looked just the same as those in the deserted settlements, but there were dogs scratching in front. I saw the tree shadows move, and a woman slowly came out into the sun. She was not at all happy at seeing the camels. As we came nearer she gathered up stones. Were these to throw at the camels if they attacked? Or to throw at her dogs if they went for me? The dogs seemed friendly enough.

She stood in my path – no one could ever accuse the Himbas of timidity. This was an old woman of the usual statuesque bearing, not a trace of fear visible on her, nor much flesh. She looked dried and polished by the sun and wind. A sudden contentment in me – I was back with these people I so admired. Suddenly I felt I must track down Kwazarane's family again.

I said a few greetings to the old lady, smiled. She chatted on and on at me, thanking me profusely for letting her see her first camel. But all the time she kept her distance from Nelson – this not helped by an unfortunate incident when a girl walked by with a water drum perched on her head, just at his eye level. Camels seemed to have achieved a legendary status since the German Camel Corps were in action; stories of the humped beasts have passed down through many generations. The woman wrapped her face in her hands, still disbelieving, and addressed Nelson, '*Engamero! Engamero!*' Oh Camel! Oh Camel! I took her hand gently, and drew it towards Andries' cheek – Andries is really the only safe bet when it comes to cuddling. The woman trusted me, though she had to pluck up courage – and when Andries bent to sniff her she did run for cover.

I sign-languaged that I was on my way north, hoping to see Ka-ada. '*Kaaa-aada*!' Immediate recognition. She took my hand now, and kissed it. I was suddenly much higher in her estimation. A friend of a friend.

Time to move on, and two youths wearing the traditional short black skirt escorted me a little way, guiding me through all the goat trails. I headed for a high pass, out of the Hoarusib and north into the Khumib Valley towards Omungunda, Wapenga and Ka-ada's last-known home. Another peculiarly hot day for the Namib – I'd imagine 42 degrees in the shade, which was the recorded temperature in Porrus yesterday. The camels in good condition, but Jan slow under all this sun.

Coming down into the Khumib at dusk I saw a lone herdsman, a young man bringing his goats into his kraal. I waved, he waved back. Then he must have realized what he was looking at. He stopped and gaped, all the time trying to keep his skirt down in a strong wind – it was a lady's acrylic scarf. I meandered a little closer to his settlement, and approached an old man. This stockman thought he'd seen it all, but his mouth dropped open, wider and wider, as he studied the camels. A young woman peeked through the spokes of a half-built hut, then, when she couldn't hold back her curiosity any longer, slipped out to have a look too. Perhaps she was a giggly woman by nature anyway, but she thought the camels were hilarious. The young man, who turned out to be her husband, also came to give his opinion on the camels. The two men leaned on their sticks, bending forward, peering at Nelson's penis, which, as in all camels, points backwards. To their delight he began urinating, always a slow process for the best of camels, and interminable with Nelson. Gasps of awe. This led, inevitably, to the question: 'How do camels mate?' My sign language was stretched to the limit.

Che-vumbowe [Ché-vum-bo-wee], the younger man, showed me a place to park the camels. '*Mei eta o té*,' I said; I'll bring some tea. This always goes down well with the Himba, as long as it's mainly sugar. It took half an hour's work to nurture the gas stove in the wind, but then I brought it over, with some tobacco, and we sat by the fire. From Che-vumbowe, I gathered that most of the nearby Himbas have spread out with the onset of the Light Rains season two weeks ago. '*Wai-pee* Ka-ada?' Where has Ka-ada gone? Great exclamations from everyone: it seems that, by an extraordinary coincidence, Ka-ada and Wapenga actually came

***Overleaf:** Nelson greeted by an Ovahimba woman. Less than one per cent of the total population of Namibia, the Himba still retain their traditional way of life, and are proud enough to want to continue eking out an existence as cattle-herders of the Namib margins.*

through this very settlement only the day before yesterday. They were riding two donkeys and were heading back to Omungunda, where I'm heading myself.

### 22 November, Orupembe district
***Midday:*** have been walking up the dry river, blasted by the sun. The temperature must surely be nearing the forties, and the riverbed offers no breeze. However, I have to stick along this route – I arranged to rendezvous with Adrian out here along the gravel bed, which is the only route the Land Rover he's obtained can cope with. If he fails to make it, he'll head to Omungunda. This will be my last supply depot.

When the wind blows, I feel I can breathe again. All morning I've been walking on the east side and that way I'm able to catch the tree shade. It's not only me that's burning up. Nelson has been appealing for a break, ramming his head into cool foliage. Or else he veers towards trees bearing mistletoe, and when I let him go over to have a snack he simply sits down in the shade. These are warnings I can't ignore – if even Nelson is tired, it's time to take note. Andries has none of his body reserves. So I've stopped here for a moment and we're dozing, squashed together under a tree.

***Night-time:*** no sign of Adrian, and towards the end of the day I ascended the terrace bank to get into the breeze. In the far distance, over at Orupembe, I see one camp fire throwing out light, like a low star. I long to be at Wapenga's fire. I realize now how much I've missed being included, sheltered. I also need to steady myself there before the final launch to the Kunene. Today I walked just over 40 kilometres through the heat. Not bad, but though the Namib is generally not a really hot desert the Hartmann Valley, beyond Omungunda, will be hotter than here. 'The Frying Pan', I call it.

### 23 November
Heading towards Omungunda, excitement gathered in me. I could almost hear the Himba goatherds spinning through the dust with the goat flocks: 'Ag! Agg! Aggg!' from Kwazarane or her equivalent. This is as close to a home as I have had in Namibia. I left them at the end of July to train the camels, and during the fifteen weeks since almost all I've done is walk or ride.

Nearing the outskirts of Onyuva, the village in front of Omungunda, we came through grasses that last time were dotted with large round tsamma melons. Old Himba huts came into view. These were vistas shown me by Kwazarane, landscapes I'd walked along with her goats. Now, though, there had been rains. It was like walking through a fresh orchard. Approaching Onyuva, I saw that one or two new structures had grown up near the kraal with its sacred fire. Not Himba huts budding from the soil but three or four alien, tin-roofed structures. Men, probably Hereros, in jeans and sunglasses lounging in front of boxes of Clansman, an alcoholic drink favoured by Himba which tastes to me like mint toothpaste. The end is nigh.

It was only the Himba men who walked forward. These were young dudes with their hair plaited in the traditional central crest; they approached proudly, with a cool swagger. I paused briefly, giving everyone time to have a good look. I recognized only one ancient man, and a woman who used to wear ochre but now had a tee-shirt warning the public not to pick up mines and bombs left from the Liberation Struggle. Then all of a sudden I spotted Ka-ada. She was among a line of middle-aged females who must have been visiting from Omungunda; they were now sitting themselves down to watch discreetly from a tree shadow.

I left the crowds and took the camels over. Ka-ada stood up, head in her hands. Supreme gratitude, it seemed like, at me having come back to her. That shiny bright face. I kissed her hand.

I introduced the camels. 'Hee!' the women said, when the camels urinated. 'Hee!' again as I got the camels to sit, showing how they fold like deckchairs.

We walked on to Omungunda. Over the last few days I'd been picturing my reunion with Wapenga – his light gait, his long arms swinging as he walked forward. However, when we came up he was sitting in the shade with a group of men smoking pipes. He stayed there as I sat the camels down. Loud roars of astonishment. Children fled. The men goggled – not just at the camels. I was a white man – how was I able to do a Himba thing, control three powerful animals? I was very proud. I knew I was really worth something in Himba eyes.

I was so busy greeting Wapenga, it took a moment to notice that a young woman to his left was smiling into my face, waiting to be acknowledged. I turned and found myself looking at Kwazarane. She looked away, now trying not to smile. I was a little taken aback: she was so pleased to see me. 'My old chum Benadiss!'

Sat down beside Wapenga, who immediately began cracking jokes at her expense. 'Kwazarane, your man has come!' That wheezing laugh of his. Then something along the lines of: 'Tonight we'll adopt him into your oruzo [patrilineal kin group] ready for the happy wedding! Tonight we'll cook up the first camel!' Kwazarane was not the slightest bit uncomfortable with this teasing. Soon she was unashamedly handing me yoghurt to swig from the gourd, and ticking me off for not wiping the brim afterwards. 'Don't worry, Kwazarane,' Wapenga said, in hysterics at his next joke, 'we'll club him if he steals away again.'

*Top: Himba women performing a strutting bird dance.*
*Above: At Omungunda, assembling supplies for the final leg of the journey.*
*Right: Kwazarane gripping a goat between her legs so that the kid might suckle.*

All this merry-making was interrupted by a voice calling from the nearest hut. It was not a Himba but a Londoner. 'Can I come out now?' Adrian crawled out through the low entrance. 'Thought I'd hide in here with the cameras. Didn't want to intrude …'

*Night-time:* I'm scribbling these notes in Kwazarane's hut; she's burning incense under a twig frame, like a lampshade, on which is spread her goatskin skirts. Already I'm losing my sense of urgency. I know I must leave the day after tomorrow, otherwise I will stay for ever and a day.

### 24 November

Adrian has gone, leaving the depot supplies. Spent the morning with Kwazarane and goats, out under the burning sun. My body needed a rest, but even so this walk was paradise.

I haven't spent much time with Ka-ada, as she's been over at Onyuva. When she did come over this morning, I noticed for the first time that her face is a little strained – apparently some sort of stomach problem. She wants to go to the hospital in Opuwo – and do those people back at home who want the Himba (and the Maasai, and the Amerindians) to remain 'unspoilt', really have the heart to deny them these things we enjoy?

*Mid-afternoon:* the camels are hobbled in the middle of the village, hopping from tree to tree, slowly robbing the settlement of its only outside shade. The Himba are very understanding – Wapenga is proud that the animals are here. Pilgrims are now arriving from afar to see the camels of his niece's friend. Old men stagger up to them, young men trot in on donkeys, women wander through with long branches of firewood perched on their heads. The general conclusion of the Himbas is that camels are like ostriches. The more you think about it, the more astute the observation is – the long neck, the body high off the sand to reduce heat, large feet, good long-distance eyes.

I've been spending a lot of time putting the camels through their paces for the crowds, and have a fairly good measure of how far I can tease the women (I think). I seize a couple of them at a time, lead them forward to touch Andries. Screams of horror and delight. And this afternoon, I finally did what I'd been leading up to all along. I grabbed Kwazarane and told her she must ride Nelson. She went to obey immediately – making me wonder why four months ago I hadn't bossed my way into her life like a Himba man. But I am not a Himba man, and can't really justify exploiting her customs for my own ends.

Everyone gathered round to see how Nelson would cope with Kwazarane. She approached slowly as I held his halter. To my horror, I saw she had total trust in me that this was safe. I began praying that Nelson wouldn't throw a tantrum and do something awful, like take a dislike to women, and toss her. When she hesitated beside the saddle, Nelson bent his head round to try to scare her. She backed off. Then, the crowds silent, she came forward resolutely, tucked her goatskin skirt between her legs and climbed aboard. I held Nelson down while she tried to make herself comfortable. She was perched with her feet high up above the stirrups, and hanging on to the saddle just with her small hands. Nelson got to his feet and I led the two of them around the village, scaring Himbas as we went.

*Dusk:* a girl has just come into Kwazarane's hut from a day in the hills. Am startled to see it's Komogunjera, who was last time just a skinny imp and used to wear two braided forelocks down over her eyes. Now, she has the status of an adolescent girl and wears plaits trailing right over her face. These form a curtain for her to look demurely through. I teased her, pretending to cut her new hair off. She flashed her eyes at me – immensely proud of her locks. Later, when we got talking a little, she pulled down her lip to show me her lower teeth – although she now has her older girl's rank, one below that of a woman, her bottom incisors haven't been bashed out yet.

Two men have agreed to ride their donkeys with me tomorrow, leading me through the hills and helping me carry the new horse-pellet sack. This is the final push, on to the Kunene. Maybe only five or six days up the Hartmann Valley, but many more if I have to swing to the western dunes to avoid stones. I've made the camels go without water today. I want them to be thirsty tomorrow at the well, when we set off to the Frying Pan. It'll be their final drink. Meanwhile, the strains of the journey are starting to tell on them. Andries, the camel that Mr Knoesen said might not last the trip, is thin but, ironically, the fittest of the lot. Nelson has a slightly raw wound on his left rear leg, suffered when charging away from flies near Porrus. Jan is the only real cause for concern. He doesn't eat. He's increasingly tetchy, nipping me this morning as I passed. He now tries all the time to work off his saddle. He has had enough.

## 25 November

*Midday:* sad farewells … The Himba think I'm doomed, being a white man. They sigh once again at my lips, which are blistered and now bleeding. Ka-ada took my hand and pressed it to her face. Then Wapenga, a hearty smile. And from Kwazarane a rather disinterested handshake but mischievous sideways glance. To the end, she's as elusive a friend as you can have.

I led the camels to the well. They did drink, but I had to be patient. As with

*Komogunjera on my return visit to the Himba, her curtain of plaits signalling her elevation in the rank (see page 30). Traditionally, two more stages follow: that of a bride, and finally, after the birth of her first child, that of a married woman.*

almost everything they do, camels have to be in the right mood. Only when I began filling all my water containers did they realize that we were all set for another march. They began drinking hurriedly.

The two youths went ahead with their donkeys, thumping them with their sticks, stopping to drink heavily from my water supply – can't comprehend that I might need it to walk a week or two without stopping. The truth is, bend as I'd like to the slow pace of the desert – its robust Himba, its robust camel – this is in the end a striving, white man's quest. The Himba, of course, would never dream of doing this journey.

I said goodbye to the two men near 'Red Drum', a navigation point to the north-east of Omungunda. They gulped two more litres of my precious water before returning home on their donkeys.

Now we are alone, just the three of us, facing the Final Push. Jan is worrying me. I know he's suffering. He's begging for water already, the end of the first day. The problem is the heat. The beetles here in the eastern Namib have waxy coats to reduce water loss, and control their temperature by raising and lowering themselves in the sand: neither option is open to us.

### 26 November

Into the Frying Pan, the lower Hartmann Valley. There was a breeze but the midday temperature must again have been about 40 degrees – rare for the Namib at any time, and it isn't summer yet. Jan began trailing, dragging at the back. I untied his rein from Andries. He needs a long holiday. Sometimes I stopped Nelson and Andries, and went back for him. I would hand-feed him with grass, and we would all stride out again. Then Jan would come forward and entwine his neck around Nelson's. It's something Nelson hates, and it's most effective.

Jan also has this uncanny way of disrupting everyday expedition procedure. This evening he's not only tipped some water over, but also rolled on to his side, rubbing the bag of horse pellets he was carrying until it was gashed open. They spilt out over the stones. Nelson spent a good hour hoovering them up.

Bumped into a vehicle sent from the Schoeman camp on the Kunene, in the hope of helping me with water. Perhaps Land Rovers can be a bit of a godsend after all … For all this, I face a serious problem with Jan. He now looks like he won't go a step further. If we continue north up the Hartmann Valley, we have four or five more days (at normal pace) through the heat. Walking in the cool of night would be risky – if the camels did for some reason bolt away into the darkness I'd never be able to track them across this gravel. Could I leave Jan here? On my arrival in a few days' time the Schoemans would help me find him by air, but judging by the difficulty the plane had last time in locating three camels even against a stark red background, it would be near impossible.

### 27 November

***Mid-morning:*** have ground to a halt. Jan worse – sitting down, hardly bothering to follow when I ignore him. Progress very slow – half a kilometre every few hours. Jan sitting beside me in a heap, like a knackered cow. My thoughts are: one, it's the heat that's now getting to him, therefore I have to get him out of here. Two, it'll be twenty days at this pace. I have water for seven or so, and the camels have no water. If I go back to the Himba it'll still take days. Three, if I leave Jan he may survive, but it's unlikely – it'll take a week before I can get someone to start looking for him. Four, I'm determined to get all three camels out of this. They're not expendable. They've earned their right to be treated as team members. Poor old Jan is looking at me now as I decide his fate. A child's trust. Not a bad camel really.

There is one other possible solution, but it's like one of those rather drastic snakebite cures that are worse than the bite. This is how it goes in theory: I cut west towards the (cooler) coast from here, weaving through the dunes (if I navigate with the GPS) along an indistinct west–east valley that André has shown me from the air. Then I head north along the beach, still in the cool wind, to the mouth of the Kunene. Here I have two choices, equally unpleasant. Either I cut back eastward, parallel with the river, through dunes of unknown severity, emerging, with luck, at the Schoeman camp on the Kunene River. Or I find a way north across the river mouth – occupied by crocodiles – into Angola, dodging the guardpost (whose soldiers have, according to Bertus, warned that they'll shoot), and cut east along the Angolan side of the river (avoiding a mountain range) to arrive at a point on the river opposite the Schoeman camp. There I call out to the camp workers, and they help me get the camels across the river into Namibia.

Ridiculous as it might seem, the second of these might be the more sensible option. Preparing for this expedition I've made files on everyone and everything – and that includes Angola. André flew me right along the border during the recce, and the dunes I'd face in the first alternative, walking back along the Namibian side of the Kunene, are monstrous. If I take the Angolan option, on the other hand, I know a possible route – it means about three or four days 'behind the lines' but I also have information about the guardpost, which is some kilometres east of the river mouth, at a bend called the Foz do Cunene. In the old days the Marxist government used to hold Unita POWs there, but now the civil war is over (almost) and the post is manned only by four soldiers. They are rarely paid, and live off the turtles they catch. Also in my favour is the moon, which by then will be perfect for night walking.

The one big disadvantage with this route is that I have to find a way across the river somehow. It looks possible from the air at both the mouth and a few kilometres inland, where there are some shallows. If I can just coax Nelson … But then, there are also the crocodiles. Rudi Loutit gave me the conservation officer's view:

'Those crocs don't take any shit from anyone.' They are large Nile crocodiles – unused to man, very territorial. André says: 'They take four Himba goats, and one Himba cow, every month.' His wife Jeanita: 'A crocodile almost took me once. I wasn't even in the river.' She was saved by a frog which jumped out of a pool, startling her and causing her to jump back from the water's edge – just as the crocodile surged.

And even if all the above anecdotes are discarded, it's a historical fact that the first descent of the Kunene, by canoe in 1965, was harried by crocodiles. Several boats have been attacked since. And during my own recce flight with André we saw a 5-metre croc lying in the river mouth. Adrian photographed it, looking like a stray timber even from 800 metres. I christened it Slick Rick.

There's yet another thing worrying me. Rudi Loutit was meant to be accompanying me, for my safety, if I entered the Skeleton Coast Park. This is the remotest stretch of Namibia – closed to the world not because there are diamonds in the sand, but because there is nothing but sand. This is a breach of trust. But I simply can't let Jan die. He is part of my expedition. Are the government worried about bad publicity? Think of the headline in *The Times*: 'Hard luck camel – he had you for breakfast.'

Sorry, we are all going to have to survive. It's now about 11 a.m. I'm turning west towards the dunes and the sea. I'll decide if I cross into Angola, or take the mountainous dune option, only when I get to the Kunene.

***Dusk:*** managed to get Jan to his feet, giving him a litre of my own drinking water and some horse pellets. He prefers heading west to north – more of a breeze on his face? Wait until he sees the dunes.

For the moment grassy gravel plains, huge smooth rock intrusions protruding into them. A hare sped off, ears up. Sometimes wild tamarisk, an olive-green bush where salty, feathery leaves are hygroscopic and absorb water from the air. But as we went on, there were fewer plants of any sort and the ground was increasingly sandy. A sense of foreboding.

Then all of a sudden I was on an escarpment edge, looking down across a new valley. And laid out rather neatly, the first dunes. They were barchans, the wandering dunes – a sequence of crescents spread out like a design on a textured carpet.

It's now two hours later. I'm camping down among the dunes. They are only 5 metres high, or twice the height of Nelson. Mere babies. Here, they look out of

***Overleaf:*** *Self-portrait in the Hartmann Valley. I tried to motivate Jan as he seriously began to weaken.*

place – they have strayed from wastelands. Further ahead, it will be us living things that are out of place.

Little prints lace around me – the feet of the hairy-footed gerbil. The sun is gone and these little nocturnal rodents will be out soon. Comforting – they are childhood friends: hamsters, guinea pigs, tortoises, gerbils … on the side of innocents.

I remember reading a translation by Amy Schoeman [stepmother of André and Bertus] of an account of an expedition by the German geologist Georg Hartmann between Angra Fria and the Kunene in September 1900. He set off south from the Kunene delta with four horses and a companion. A storm gathered, sands rose into the air – 'One can see barely five yards ahead'. The two men lost one horse, then another – however hard he beat them, they refused to go on. Halfway to Angra Fria – 'we can hardly stand' – he cut east, the opposite direction from where I'm now heading. He lost another horse somewhere on the way. To get some peace from the tormenting sand the men were reduced to sticking their heads in holes in the ground. When the storm died, and they at last emerged not far from where I'm presently sitting, the final horse, 'the dapple-grey Hans', was too thirsty to eat.

But I must concentrate on the present. From all I remember, Hartmann's route was less sandy than mine. Nor must I think forward to my quandary at the river mouth – even worse dunes or else Angola. Poor Nelson is carrying 160 kilos – more than his fair share. Andries also weakening – tugging at his rope, and sitting down whenever I pause. First time ever that he's shown signs of wilting, though I've always been careful to nurture his young body. If he goes into decline, the end will follow quickly. Jan continues to be nasty, swiping at me if I give him the chance – which I don't often. Is he in pain? I suspect so. Nelson not exactly happy. Behind us he sees grass. Ahead he sees only sand. How far will his trust in me last? One day? Two days into the dunes?

I have given Jan another 3 litres of my own water. It will encourage him, but do little for his strained metabolism. And I cannot risk more – what good is it to him if I kick the bucket? A leader's duty is sometimes to safeguard himself – sounds like a line from an SAS survival manual.

***Night-time:*** I'm full of doubts – thought the desert was meant to have made me resilient. Just as I've feared they might one day, thoughts of home are sapping my will. A good person's death suddenly seems to make any of my achievements in life seem pointless. Mum came, went – and what? It's all so futile if you don't have a faith – in God's purpose, I suppose I mean. But what true researcher or explorer has faith in anything? Our very job is to question, to doubt, to uncover the truth – not trust in Jesus, Mohammed, or own Western science. In theory at least, we've been dispatched out here to dispel all the dreams and nightmares people have back home – it's our duty, and it's also our only justification for going uninvited to remote parts.

Second boots have died. Now on to canvas deck shoes. Have only my day clothes and my night clothes – and my day clothes are stiff with salt encrusted from my sweat. Actually starting to scratch me.

### 28 November

***Dawn:*** feel better this morning. I'll carry on west through the dunes. I can make this decision easily, looking the desert square in the face. For all last night's nagging thoughts, I do believe I'm all the stronger for having been exposed out here.

***Mid-morning:*** nonetheless, set off in some trepidation. I had negotiated yesterday's dunes, but from here on they'd get bigger, more meddlesome. We set off, and all too soon, there they were, straddling the horizon, blocking me out, linking arms. Worst thing was – and still is, as I write – that I'm not sure if anyone has actually crossed through here alone before. By vehicle it's obviously impassable, and it isn't yet clear if it's passable by camel. 'A definite valley,' André concluded as we flew over much earlier. Could have fooled me.

I was navigating now with occasional reference to my GPS – for all the good it did me. Although my readings told me I had flown over exactly this route, I recognized not a single feature. In the end it was up to the desert, not me or my instruments – I could wind west through the sands only as and when they let me.

Now, three hours on, I've stopped for a breather. I feel dwarfed, Nelson feels dwarfed – a plaything, toy of the natural forces. Nearby a second ago, the shovel-nosed lizard, or Namib sand-diver, was doing a dance specially adapted for these sands – lifting its feet two at a time to keep the heat off.

***Midday:*** for a while there were granite crests in the sands, smooth boulder crops, a lone crag – all these were signs of hope, anchors in a moving sea. But now I've entered the dune fields proper – serious, grown-up dunes squatting in front of me. And more and more in ranks behind. Sand waves now also blocking me in on all sides, closing off exits.

I've sat down to give Jan a rest. He keeps tugging at the back – I've tied him on to the caravan again because I'll lose him forever if he drops behind in this dune maze. Andries is scared – pulling back Nelson, trying to stop him obeying me. Nelson also beginning to stop now. Every now and again I have to turn to him and give him a good talking to. So far, these are only temporary halts – like warnings. Every minute I'm bluffing Nelson, acting as if I do have control over whether he comes or not – as if at a flick of my fingers I can summon Tommy or Adrian to help me. For now, I tell the camels aloud that it's going to be all right. They take comfort from my voice. I hum, I skip, I jolly them along. And they follow me up another rise, and then see yet another ridge of sand appearing, and another. Every step goes deeper into the wasteland and further away from food. One day, Nelson will call my bluff and stop. And then what?

*Later:* the dunes changed shape, turned into long angry hills kicking out towards us. I led the camels along these ridges. Up and down. It was never apparent to me where the sand lay soft and would give way under our feet, or where it was firm. If firm, Nelson would follow. If soft, he would not. It was very simple – and again I knew I was pushing the odds. In the Namib-Naukluft Park I used to bring Jan forward, get him to lead us through the soft patches. Now Jan was useless, a burden. Instead I had to leave all the camels and walk forward, feeling the ground for softness. It was like working a minefield with a detector.

By late afternoon the air was cool and moist – at last the moderating effect of the sea. Soon – today, tomorrow – we might smell the salt as well. Or maybe not. There might be one firm, gently rising dune between us – ten minutes' work – or twenty impassable Berlin Walls.

Walking, walking. My legs were still holding up in the soft sand, but Nelson's rear legs were weakening. Once we saw ahead a spring, a pool of water with an algal-like rim, almost eclipsed by the dunes. Nelson ran at it, throwing me aside. But already I could see it was saline. Not one animal footprint had dented the mud surround.

This would go on forever, it seemed. Sand mounds, mountains. I couldn't believe how loyal Nelson had been to me. I began congratulating him on every dune rise. At last I felt I could say, 'Not long now, Nelson, not long now' – a phrase I used at the close of each day's walk.

Ahead, a bright light – the dying sun shimmering off low cloud, I thought at first. But it became apparent as we walked that the light was glimmering off a moving surface. The sea. We had virtually broken through, and in fact I had been looking at the Atlantic for some ten minutes.

I pressed on until last light. I wanted the camels to know we were out of the dunes. The final slope, down on to the beach flats: together, we ran all the way to the bottom. And then all four of us stopped dead. Because this wasn't a very nice place at all. With its tearing wind and cold it was like a science fiction film set depicting somewhere inhospitable like Jupiter. I began to wish I was back in the dunes. The monotonous flats were broken only by low black rock extrusions, mere ruffles which provided no shelter from the flying sands. A ghastly place even for a strandwolf – the hyena that looks like a werewolf. And with a sandstorm brewing up, just like poor old Georg Hartmann's.

So here I am, sheltering behind the saddles and shivering. I'm about 50 kilometres north of where the *Dunedin Star*'s passengers waited for rescue on the beach. Did they have weather like this? I think not. Grit is firing like shotgun pellets in the wind. Even the camels are suffering, and they're built for this. Sand up my nose and under my eyelids. All is miserable. Tomorrow I must proceed up the coast to the Kunene mouth. Hope the camels can stand it. Hope I can. The map – not usually prone to outpourings of melodrama – calls this 'Seekus van die Dood', the Coast of the Dead.

# 11

# A STROLL ALONG 'THE COAST OF THE DEAD'

**29 November, 12 kilometres south of the Kunene mouth**
**Night-time:** a few days ago, I asked for the 'moderating coolness' of the coast. Now I've got it. The wind fleecing me with cold sand. I'm sheltering behind a giant hummock knitted together by a meagre salt bush – the sand has been stopped in its relentless progress up the coast by something that looks almost dead with the effort. Now Nelson is finishing it off. Other signs of life? Forget it. Even the beach ghost crabs have hidden in the sand until it's bearable.

Walked exactly 40 kilometres to here, blown by the wind, fired by the sand. We were hardly able to turn our heads, and even Jan showed little inclination to stop and die out here. I weakened as I walked without eating – even pausing to take a swig of water from Andries' saddlebag meant risking being left behind by the camels. Later I managed to snatch a can of meat while Nelson dragged me onward. I even had to urinate while walking.

My map was right: Coast of the Dead it is. You feel that, if you keel over, your body will be mummified on the spot. Passed a dead Cape cormorant – desiccated, but intact. You get the feeling it's just a sample.

As usual, no possibility in this wind of lighting the stove to make tea. For what must be forty days and forty nights I've wandered in the wilderness eating unheated tins of meatballs for supper. I need the energy, but forty cans must be near the human limit.

*Having reached the bleak Seekus van die Dood, 'Coast of the Dead',*
*Andries had finally had enough. He walked away, then lost his nerve and stopped, waiting for*
*Jan and Nelson to follow.*

Nelson's big day tomorrow. If only he understood the importance of crossing either the river or the dunes. What would I promise him if he agreed to do it? Never-ending supply of his thistles. I'll approach the river slowly, check for sheer dunes/crocs/troops. We'll see.

**30 November**
**Mid-morning:** I'm pausing to take stock. Ahead, very near now, the Kunene, the river to which I've been heading for over three months, the target on which I've fixed my sights for a year. But now it doesn't matter … Any fool can get to their objective and kill their team while doing it. They must pull through with me. And look what I'm facing: to the east, my right, mountainous dunes; to the west, the South Atlantic; to the north, Angola – have I mentioned the minefields? Perhaps I'm being alarmist – it's 'generally thought' they start further over to the east.

Got up late again this morning (6 a.m.). A terrible, sand-blasted night. Not at all enjoying the luxury of no blistering heat. Bothered in the night by a jackal. He removed the rubbish sack, taking it off to a dune rise to undertake a thorough investigation. Clanged the cans for an hour. When this proved unsatisfactory, came back and snuffled around me for something better. Hovered only at arm's distance – just out of reach, like one of those tropical mosquitoes that, in the Amazon, elusively buzz right by your ear. Ruined my night. And I do need sleep to be able to think clearly. No one in the world even knows where I am, precisely.

Progressed north along the coast, the wind picking up steadily again. Paused by a hefty whale vertebra, lying like a beached tree base. Occasional sailing ship masts lying around. People died out here – people unrecorded by history, people who were perhaps as resolute and fit as I am. But I hold the edge – Nelson.

**At the Kunene, evening:** soon we were seeing the sandy flats that must signify the delta. Nothing picturesque, just mud and a sand bar. But it was the Kunene … My great moment: 'Sound the trumpets, I've achieved my goal!' But it meant nothing. We were a long way from home.

Although the army post was well inland and on the other (Angolan) bank, I hobbled the camels half a kilometre south of the river, out of sight. Then I went inland to inspect the dune option. I didn't walk very far. The dunes looked diabolical – a towering, pallid hill range concealing heaven knows what tricks. I turned back to inspect the mouth's possible crossing points. Slowly I walked up towards the water, but there was no sign of soldiers on the far bank – no sign, even, of Slick Rick. [Conceivably the crocs had been disturbed by scientists who were in the region investigating the consequences of placing the dam upriver at

Epupa.] Then closer, right to the edge of the delta. Of the two crossing points I'd noted from the air, the one at the mouth, where I'd seen the crocodile, had been the most promising. From the ground, however, it looked a dire prospect. The Kunene was over a metre deep and choppy, the sea knocking up against the oncoming river. I saw immediately that there was no possibility of crossing – and judging by the exposed sandbanks, we were almost at low tide. I gazed, miserably, across the mouth. It was less than 40 metres wide, with scores of giant green turtles swimming in it. And tantalizingly close on the other side were the crinkled rock flats of Angola.

Half-heartedly I filmed the turtles as they stuck up their parrot-beak faces, glanced around blindly as they took in air, and ducked down. This could have been a great moment, being silent with turtles in the back of beyond. The outside world talked of the turtles as monsters – John van Bergen's father, a fisherman, had said that some of them were armed with long talons. Very possibly they were, but turtles were the last thing I was interested in right now. Sullenly I walked upriver towards the only other crossing point, stopping only when I bumped into an enormous male Cape fur seal. He was basking, fast asleep, a mound of sleek fat, without a care in the world – not even of Slick Rick. Perhaps, like Andries, he lived his life in blissful ignorance.

Came to the reed clump which was my marker for the shallows. It reeked of something fishy, and had the undeniable hallmarks of a crocodile patch. The mud was flattened and scored – you could see the giveaway trail left by the tail. But this was a small crocodile – a metre or so. Looking upriver along the opposite bank, I could make out the Angolan guardpost perched above the river at the Foz do Cunene. I ascended a small dune and used my camera's telephoto lens to search for signs of any soldiers. With so many reeds it was difficult to be absolutely sure no one was there, but anyway how often would a forgotten outpost bother to patrol one of the remotest river banks in Africa? I turned my attention to the river itself. Studied the shallows, fans of brown mud which showed through the blue water. I memorized their pattern, and went down to the bank.

I looked again along the Angolan bank. All clear – as far as I could see. No harm in giving the waters a tentative try – after all, the seal had been all right in the river. Besides, the only other option was those dunes. I would take it slowly, restricting myself to clear water.

I stepped into the Kunene at last and began following the mudbank shallows. So far, the river was less than half a metre deep. I reached an exposed mudbank, midstream. So far, so good. I went further. And then further. At last I found I was at the far bank. The water had been thigh deep at the worst. Well, well, I thought,

**Above:** *The Nile crocodiles
(Crocodylus niloticus) of the
Kunene are the stuff of adventure
books. In 1965, canoeist Willem van
der Riet and Gordon Rowe
navigated the Kunene from its source
in Angola, surviving not only
starvation but also the notorious
crocodiles, which snapped at their
paddles as they went by.*

**Left:** *The sands of the Namib are
abruptly interrupted from moving
north by the Kunene River. Unable
to cross the deep water into Angola,
the camels and I were forced to cross
these sands parallel to the river.*

199

as realization of what I'd done rose in me. I was standing in Angola. Suddenly I was jubilant. I wouldn't have to face those dunes! I ran off to fetch the camels.

Success would all depend on Nelson. I must try the crossing just after he'd had that first drink from the river – the camels would be over-excited, full of that strange energy which the thought of water gives them. In their excitement they'd shove forward right into the river. Before he knew it, Nelson would have lost his fear of the soft sand.

I put the plan into action. At the water I had the usual battle to keep them under control. Then, hardly able to control my own excitement, let alone theirs, I tied Jan and Andries to Nelson and led him forward into the shallows. He came, stamping his feet in the water, his eyes on the reedy far bank. All three camels were following me like happy dogs on a leash – anything was bliss after a dose of those dunes. This was easier than I could ever have expected. I was already almost at the far side. Not a sign of a crocodile, no protest from the camels. But, only two steps from the Angolan bank, I stopped. What was I doing? I was about to step into a gun-happy country which was only now emerging from civil war. I'd never expected to get across so easily. Now that I was suddenly here, I felt uneasy. Had I thought everything through? I'd hurried here with the camels just a little too quickly. In thirty seconds' time, the moment I stepped ashore, I'd be on the run. In Angola for at least three days. Better to be on the safe side, check all my equipment, ready myself properly.

I turned the camels around in the river, and we came all the way back. Set up camp, out of sight, in the cover of the dunes. And here I am now, thinking things through. It does look like Nelson can handle the crossing – even his pet phobia, the soft sand – and judging by the stick markers I've placed in the bank the water level is still falling rapidly. I shall rise at 4.30 a.m. and be ready to cross at first light. I estimate it should be low tide then. With any luck, unpaid soldiers don't rise for a dawn patrol through the middle of nowhere. I think my chances of being caught are extremely low. And these dunes look terrible – higher than anything I've yet tackled. The only other choice is to retreat the way I came, losing Jan. Don't ever want to retrace my footsteps – either in my life, or here.

*1 December*
***Mid-morning, south bank:*** Disaster. Rose in the dark and saddled up fast to catch the tide. At first light, leaving the camels hidden, went to inspect the river bank. And found it engulfed by water. At first I was confused: I must have got the tides wrong. Did some quick sums – no, surely not. Then this was floodwater – released from the inland dams that control the Kunene's flow many, many

kilometres from here. I stared in disbelief, the water still rising in front of my eyes, my exit door being closed in my face.

What to do now? Now the water was thick with sediment and running fast. And across the river, something caught my eye. A man walking through the reeds. A soldier? Only a scientist? I reached for my video camera, trained the telephoto on the man, but he was gone.

I walked back to the camp and sat with the camels. For once they were raring to go. They must feel that the journey's end can't be long now. So I'm here in the camp, and the camels are all loaded up and waiting, wondering what's wrong. A gerbil has popped out, and now a second, both questing after leftover muesli.

In one way, the decision is made easy. Crossing the river is out of the question. It's simply too high. That leaves the dunes. But I'm not mentally geared up to tackle all that sand. Need to adjust to the idea. I studied an old German map once, and Hartmann made a crossing somewhere near here – but where? And how long did it take him? And with how many people? I shall be doing the crossing like him, blind. But with only camel team-mates.

*Midday:* just now, something unexpected. A plane suddenly in the air overhead. I realized immediately: André. How long had he been searching? I jumped into action, hand-signalling. First with crossed forearms, then pointing to the river – i.e. 'I can't do the crossing'. Second, pointing sharply east. I was heading through the dunes. He waggled his wings. He understood.

He flew over a second time. A message dropped from the sky on a streamer. It was weighted by two cartons of blackcurrant juice, both of which shattered. It gave me the tide times, advised me about the Epupa dam research team being here, and wished me luck.

I'm keeping the camels saddled, letting them graze while I watch the river, hoping it'll fall so that I don't have to cross those dunes. Soon, at 4 p.m., it's low tide, but the river is still rising from floodwater. Perhaps it's just as well. How would my poor Dad feel? Alone on Christmas Day, the anniversary of Mum's death – and with his son in a tropical prison?

Strategy: we walk till we drop. No messing about. Dawn to dusk. Camels have only one kilo of horse pellets left each – a fifth of their normal daily allowance. And no water. I must bully Jan through this last hurdle. It's perhaps a 40-kilometre dune belt. I have 40 litres of water – ample for myself for five days – and 10 litres for Jan. That's 2 litres a day, not enough to keep his metabolism hydrated, but it'll help him ingest any grazing we find. If we get stuck out there, I can't be sentimental: I drink his water ration.

***Dusk, somewhere in the dunes:*** even after having made the decision to head for the dune mountain I found myself dragging my feet, letting the camels have a last feed, willing the river to drop. Finally it was 4 p.m., low tide. I allowed myself a final glance at the level. As high as ever. No last-minute reprieve from the dunes. I let the camels take one final drink and have one final nibble of sea wheat, then I turned to face the sand.

Hardly able to believe I was attempting it, I led the camels towards the steep rise of sand which ascended abruptly from the river just opposite the guardpost. I took the slope gently, trying not to frighten them. We climbed and climbed – Andries yanking back, Jan sitting down. All three camels looked resentful.

Higher and higher in the dusk. By zigzagging up the dune, winding south and north, south and north, we trailed up and up above the river bank. If this had been only sand, it might perhaps have been a dune higher even than those near Sossusvlei, some of the highest in the world. However, the sand here seemed to be only a layer of dunes covering a hill range. Not that this necessarily made it any easier – what counted was the number of dead ends, steep waves, curves and eccentric tucks.

Now down below me was the Foz do Cunene, the guardpost. There were two soldiers bent over – cleaning boots? – and two white people, scientists presumably, standing by a large tent. Beyond them, the grey rocklands of Angola, the tail end of the Namib desert, all hazy in the windblown dust. Then as we moved onward the view was gone, swallowed up, like us, by the sand. We arched back and forward, trying different sand ridges, different slipfaces, always mindful that we might enter a trap – a sink hole of soft sand. Once, I thought we were caught. We found ourselves in a trough, loose sand on all sides. I tried every slope, pulling Nelson north, south, east, west. Finally he gave up trying. He just stood there. I turned and shouted at him. He backed off – this powerful animal terrified by me. He roared and roared, refusing to do anything. I had to calm him again, tell him I was sorry. After a dignified pause he walked straight up out of the pit.

We are now camped in a hollow. No time to choose the site carefully, but there are occasional blades of gemsbok grass. The camels too tired to wander and eat, so I've been gathering it by hand for them. We've walked only a couple of hours, and it was harrowing for all three camels. Tonight, their last food from me.

Progress not too bad – 7 kilometres from the Foz? So far, vague dune streets have been running to the east. I've been lucky. Must do 15 kilometres tomorrow. If not, turn back. Will the camels cope? Jan does need his hols. He's not much better than he was in the Hartmann Valley but he's more reluctant to give up right out here.

***2 December***

***Dawn:*** in the night gerbils rattled about my camp, dodging in and out of the saddles. All round me this morning, their tracks. They're thriving off the seeds of the dune lucerne. Just now I went on a reconnoitre ahead, to plot out a route. Excitement: there's a view – no high-rise dune obstructions, just steep hillocks. Trouble is, the wrong type of hillock, the type with walls, can be as obstructive as a mountain.

***2 p.m.:*** no wind at all. Copious sweating. The cool sea breeze eliminated here by the sheltering, cooking dunes. Jan had to be tugged and heaved for the first three hours. Eventually I let him loose. Feared he might just sit down, stretch out and wait to die. However, he is still following – though waits until we are out of sight behind the next dune. Then he loses his nerve. He still cares enough to try to live.

At last I'm being stretched, living off my senses. I dread these moments on expeditions but, rather perversely, I need times when I'm up against it. Because 'it' is in part what we should be trying to explore. I believe it's only when we're fighting hard, when our senses are sharpened and we're animally alive, that humans can start to relearn what it's like to be a part of natural processes, the ones that make existence tick. The experience of our ancestors surviving in the wild. Essentially, every expedition I have ever done has been a search for this lost connection. Why is that search important to me? Because it seems to me that, unless we can discover how we are placed in relation to these eternal, God-like forces, we shall never know if what we do in our lives is actually pointless. And why is that search important to anyone else? Because, whether we are city bankers or production-line workers, fundamentally we are all explorers. Our questing nature is what marks us out as human.

***Mid-afternoon:*** have been making good progress and starting to relax a little. Am allowing myself all the water I want to drink. Also giving Jan 2 litres. Presently, I'm resting for a moment. No shade, just the hot sands. Had to dig a bit to find ground that was cool enough to sit on. But at this rate – and there's no guarantee 'this rate' will continue – I will be out of the dunes tomorrow. From tonight, if all goes well, I can afford to be softer on Jan. I can slow down, nurse him through.

***Dusk:*** we have done well – 20 kilometres today? Though one incident threatened to scupper all of us. Nelson, losing his nerve before descending a slope, shied to the side and somehow entangled his saddle in Andries' halter. For a moment they tugged at each other. Then both tumbled to the ground. Nelson roared bitterly at Andries, Andries bellowed back. Nelson very angry, apparently blaming him entirely. Andries frightened – not least because his head was under Nelson's armpit, pinned to the ground, his mouth filling with sand. Nelson yanked and yanked, entirely uninterested in Andries' predicament. I dived into the thick of it and eventually was able to undo Andries' halter. He sprang free, but the thick iron rings had been distended. Wasted half an hour scraping the sand in an attempt to find my knife, which had disappeared in the scuffle.

Don't know how much further the dunes extend, but they must be ending shortly. Tomorrow, or the next day, I will come over a dune rise and see grass again. Then level ground. Success is in the breeze – a sweet smell.

### 3 December, Kunene, 1.5 kilometres south of the Schoeman camp, final destination

Woke feeling good, after delicious but inconsequential dream about a girl I used to know – probably now married/mortgaged. Before the camels and I were away, a swarm of bees descended on us. Apparently they were after any spare salt and moisture. They clustered around the saddles, so thick I began to think they were wanting to build a hive. The camels not disturbed much – too exhausted. But I had to saddle up in slow motion to avoid aggravating the bees – the last thing I wanted to do today was die from a camel stampede.

The dune streets carried me directly east. Then, only half an hour's walk from last night's camp, we came up a rise from where I could discern a peak. It was grey and sharp, undoubtedly too angular for sand. This hilltop was beyond the dunes, east-north-east, perhaps only 10 kilometres away. Walked on, and the horizon opened up further. A range of tattered mountains – undoubtedly on the Angolan side of the river. However, the important thing just now was that I was getting a view at all – we were almost clear of the dunes. Perhaps 5 kilometres to go. Nelson began to speed up: he couldn't take his eyes off the horizon.

A warm feeling in my tummy as I began to realize we were going to make it. Very little could stop us – as long as we continued keeping our nerve through the loose sands. I slowed the camels down. Gave Jan the remainder of his water and some of mine – 8 litres total.

Aimed down a dune street. And beneath our feet, step by step, the sand became firmer. Grasses seemed to pluck up courage, clumps sprang up around us. The view opened. We stopped, and in front of us lay a sweeping grass valley – the top of the Hartmann. Larks filling the air over it. I could also make out large birds – Ludwig's bustard plodding about in the valley. The beginning of the end …

We walked on, then had to stop again. Nelson had suddenly realized he was passing food. He began rapidly working through the grass clumps, one after the other. Andries was soon doing the same. Jan was too dazed from tiredness to eat, and only grazed after I'd hand fed him a while. I looked about while the camels chewed. Near at hand, male mountain chats, black and white little birds, hopping about. Fleets of grey-backed finch larks sweeping the grasses. Further away to my right, a small group of Rüppell's korhaan – their long, thin, tubular necks protruding from the grasses as they walked about open-mouthed, thin beaks ajar to cool themselves.

Paradise, you'd think. But this didn't feel right. I was meant to be triumphant. The sands were fading away, we were safely near a major river. But I had no longing to leave the desert. After three months my team had become a solid little band. I wasn't so sure I wanted to rejoin the world – here we had our own.

I thought of Thomas Hardy: man, 'the only blot on an otherwise kindly universe.' People were always making a mess of things. The desert is more or less unsullied, its colours clean, its sinuous curves unbroken, its processes uninterrupted. I'd adapted a little to its ways. Even to the heat and the dust. Being fried and tired didn't seem to matter that much. There were greater rewards.

We walked on. The camels began to accelerate again. We swung through the valley past granite lumps the size of apartment blocks, and linked up to the Schoemans' vehicle trail. Over severe hills and down again into the river's ravine, to the very brink of the water's edge, just downriver from the Schoeman camp. In the last light, unable to find a way there through the sheer hills, made my own camp for the last time. By the water I saw a squad of helmeted guineafowl, pecking along the river after their evening drink. And two pied crows – faithful followers, or so they seem, until the end.

I haven't let the camels drink. Not until tomorrow, and we've done the last 1.5 kilometres. Then I'll believe we're safe for certain, and I can risk the mayhem – three thirsty camel desperadoes sighting a cool drink. Now, I'm writing by moonlight. Poignant: last night alone together. Nelson beside me, trying to drink my tea. Jan breathing heavily behind, Andries looking on, anxious – thinks he might be missing out. They don't know it's all over. The desert took us in, and we have emerged the other side. But I won't later speak of having conquered it. Why do explorers talk about 'conquering' deserts, mountains, rivers? The natural elements will always endure. The best we can ever do is play a small part in their scheme of things.

## 4 December

**Dawn:** woke this morning to see the river acacias rich green, the cool water running thick and silver, like mercury. At last it's sinking in: I have done it. We have

**Left:** *Water had to be brought to the desperate camels to keep them away from the river and its crocodiles (*Crocodylus niloticus*). After a few days, however, Jan managed to break away from me and plunged in. Totally new to deep water, he was soon bellowing, eyes rolling in fear, and had to be dragged out. After all that the other camels and I had been through in the desert for Jan, we'd almost lost him to a river.*

**Above:** *My professional colleagues: Jan, Andries and Nelson.*

done it. Despite my fears, despite the warnings of people who know the desert better than me. The end of my three-and-a-half-month walk. Today I will be able to dance, to sing. Be able to call up Adrian, tell him – is he still in Namibia? – that I'm safe. And the word will eventually work its way to Dad. And then I'll radio Bertus or André – and thank them and thank them and thank them for their faith in me.

Now my short walk around the hills to the final Schoeman camp. I should get a good reception. Nelson and I are a little piece of history.

***Otja Camp, Kunene:*** walked slowly into the camp, a vegetated stretch of river bank. Frogs in choruses, pigeons. Little tents pitched on grass that's mown by Himba cattle. Soaring all around are the rocks of Namibia and Angola, the two countries divided by this glassy, fast river, the Kunene. Crocs 2 and 3 metres long occasionally slipping by in the muddy current. I wondered how I would have tackled them if I'd arrived now at the other bank, through the stark hill ranges of Angola.

The camp workers drifted out, cautiously. I must have been grinning right across my face, but no one was grinning back. 'Hasn't André said I'd be coming? My name is Benedict.' There was no response. I saw the man was grimacing at the camels, concentrating on keeping his distance. 'Oh, that's only Nelson,' I said. Some smiles as other camp workers assembled now – they seemed to take comfort in numbers. And one man did at last come to shake my hand – but not exactly a standing ovation. He then just signalled me to a tent – eyes still warily on those camels – and indicated a good patch of grazing a little way off. Women emerged from a Himba hut and did now skip forward, but it was only to gape and sigh at the camels. They made themselves comfortable to watch as I unloaded. It was all a bit of a let-down.

I am of course grateful: Jan safe, Nelson safe, Andries safe, Benedict safe. I have an excitement swelling within me – I have done what I set out to do, and can go home. In a few days André will fly in with Jeanita, with whom (as well as Save the Rhino) the camels will soon be living. She will begin to get to know them for herself, and in turn she will fall in love with them, and I will be happy for her.

But there is another half of me, and this feels deflated. The desert didn't bring me to my knees as most told me it would. In fact, all I want to do at this moment is to head back there. We had something – and it's already beginning to slip away. What was it? Something to do with the dimensions of the desert. Space to breathe, to expand – released from Western baggage, the technology that runs our world at home and but here failed so miserably to keep up. The camels, by contrast, were able to be part and parcel of the desert. And by accommodating something of their rhythm, their dogged outlook, I was able to get very close to freedom, a condition we in the West all seek, but have lost the ability to attain.

*Midnight:* can't sleep. Keep waking under the moonlight and thinking something's wrong. But it's simply that there are no camels by my side. No munchings, no snufflings. Nor Nelson's head slowly descending out of the darkness to be near mine.

# *12*

# A BRIEF HISTORY OF NAMIBIA

## FIRST AFRICANS

For well over a million years hunter-gatherers have wandered the rocks, sands and grasses of the country we now know as Namibia. They left stone axes, cleavers and rock shelters scattered behind, but few other clues. However, sites dating from 30,000 years ago are attributed to the San-speaking peoples known to us simply as 'Bushmen'. It seems that the Bushmen were not then restricted to the desert, as today, but were once the sole occupants of the whole of southern Africa.

By some 2000 years ago Namibia's Bushmen were gradually being displaced from the south by ancestors of the modern Nama (Hottentot), who spoke a Khoi 'click' language (named after one of its characteristic sounds), were also yellow-skinned and perhaps had a close origin; and by the Damara, who spoke a similar Khoi language but were dark-skinned. But it was the arrival 1500 years ago of Bantu-speaking true farmers from south-central Africa which was to have the greatest impact on the region. They brought with them not only their herds but metal-working tools and pottery, forcing the Damaras and Namas south and the fully nomadic Bushmen into the desert margins. Soon, the Afrikaner *trekkers* from the south were also to dispossess the Bushmen. The sorry remains of their communities are still to be found in the Kalahari, but elsewhere they survive only in the genes of other tribes who bedded their women.

## FIRST EUROPEANS

The first European in the region was the fifteenth-century Portuguese navigator Diego Cão, who was dispatched by King John II to establish a maritime route for the eastern spice trade around the African Cape. The explorer's two caravels sailed down the west coast of the continent through uncharted waters beyond the Congo, beyond Angola, but the land continued doggedly south. By December 1485 Cão had reached the desert shore of Namibia and was ready to give up and go home. He got as far as a rocky promontory now called Cape Cross, and stayed only long enough to erect a stone padrão, or cross, before turning back for Portugal.

Another Portuguese explorer, Bartolomeu Diaz, who did succeed in finding the route around the Cape, stopped by in 1487. He anchored at Walvis Bay and also took shelter in Angra Pequena, later Lüderitz. Generally, though, this extremely uninviting desert was ignored until the eighteenth century – and even then interest in the country was restricted to its shoreline potential. Whalers began working the plankton-rich seas, seal hunters gathered pelts, traders dug for guano. In 1793 the Dutch authorities, wishing to secure their hold on the Cape, sent a vessel up the African coast to annex the only deepwater harbour, Walvis Bay – a port taken over by the British just two years later when they occupied the Cape settlement.

## EUROPEANS ENTER THE INTERIOR

Up until now, the only accounts of the interior were coming from leathery-skinned missionaries or traders. No European power had been fussed about bagging this desolate patch of sand and dust. This was a shame, as it was eventually to see the world's most spectacular diamond rush.

Nonetheless, by the early nineteenth century the first European ripples were being felt inland. The Bastas, descendants of indigenous Hottentot women and the Dutch Cape settlers of the early seventeenth century, came under increasing pressure from the white farmers advancing inland from the Cape, and in 1868 migrated over the Orange River into Namibia. At the same time, the Namas were on the move north. Equipped with horses and guns and using guerrilla tactics learnt from the Boer farmers, the Nama chief Jonker Afrikaner quashed the other indigenous Namas and the Damaras and (Bantu) Hereros of the central north. Over the next few decades, conflict followed conflict. English, German and Finnish missionaries called on their respective governments to colonize Namibia to stop all the killing and enslavement. However after 1884, when Germany did announce its annexation of Namibia, their troops were to witness some of the worst bloodshed yet. This time, they did the blood letting themselves.

A German tobacco merchant, Adolf Lüderitz, was the man who had first seriously attracted Berlin's attention to Namibia. Almost alone in the European world, he thought he could see a future out here. If he could set up a trading settlement, his thinking went, then colonization and potential opportunities might follow. In April 1883 an expedition sent on his behalf landed with ox carts and tents at the barren, empty bay of Angra Pequena. Within a month, contact was made with missionaries administering to the apparent spiritual needs of the Namas at Bethanie. Chief Josef Fredericks agreed to sell the land for £100 and two hundred rifles. This purchase was followed by that of a coastal strip north from the Orange River. Lüderitz asked Otto von Bismarck, the Chancellor, for protection. The Germans felt they had rather missed out in the 'Scramble for Africa' and very soon, in August 1884, the frigates *Leipzig* and *Elisabeth* were proudly raising the German flag at the (admittedly rather godforsaken) settlement. The next year, still unaware of the diamonds that lay unnoticed, glinting by moonlight across his wasteland purchase, Lüderitz went down with his ship in violent Skeleton Coast seas.

## GERMAN CONSOLIDATION

Britain and Germany met at the Berlin Conference of 1900, and agreed – with a series of rather-too-neat lines on maps – on the exact division of the southern African spoils. Britain would get Bechuanaland, present-day Botswana, to the east, and keep Walvis Bay.

In the absence of Lüderitz, the Germans began consolidating their hold on South West Africa, this unlikely dry territory they had acquired. In 1890 they erected a fortress at Windhoek and in 1893 the Schutztruppe, or Defence Force, set to work building landing facilities at Swakopmund to facilitate the arrival of the first German farmers.

As the settlers spread their cattle herds over the land, Major Theodor von Leutwein tried, with only four companies of soldiers, to conclude peace treaties up and down the country with inter-warring tribes, and to ban weapons and alcohol. On 12 January 1904 the Hereros rebelled, clubbing to death 123 of the invading farmers and chasing away their cattle. Reinforcements from Germany came in the form of General von Trotha and a whole division of troops. The Herero had spared women and children, but von Trotha doesn't seem to have had any such intention. The Hereros gathered their families at Waterberg to make a stand. They were unable to hold the ground, and more than half the population died in a bloodbath. The survivors retreated east, staggering into the *sandveld* of the Kalahari, many fading even before they reached this pitiless land.

All this time the Bantu-speaking Ovambos remained isolated in the densely populated north, largely unaware of their status as subjects of a German colony. Following such extensive Herero losses the Ovambos now composed about half of Namibia's black population, and it was they who would inherit power when independence and 'one man one vote' finally came the way of the protectorate. It was still a long way off.

## SOUTH AFRICAN RULE

German rule came to an end during the First World War, when the Union of South Africa sided with the British and quickly overran the heavily outnumbered German force, which surrendered on 9 July 1915. The following year the Allied Powers authorized South Africa to administer the territory as an 'integral part' of their own country, though the mandate government was, in the course of time, charged with the responsibility of guiding the territory to independence.

The land had already seen a migration of white Boers from South Africa, but the administration now began adding to the numbers of Afrikaners with a deliberate settlement programme. Following the Second World War, in defiance of the United Nations, Pretoria tried to incorporate the territory into South Africa, making it a fifth province. All movement and settlement was subject to the restrictions of apartheid.

In the 1960s the South West Africa People's Organization (SWAPO) – initially a labour organization for the Ovambos – became identified as the main force of resistance to the South African presence. When SWAPO elected to pursue an armed struggle, thousands of young Namibians fled to organize resistance from abroad. They found allies next door, in the Marxist government of Angola. This set in motion years of costly (for South Africa) guerrilla warfare along the Angola–Namibia border. The situation was compounded by the superpowers – the USSR backing Angola's communist MPLA government, via the Cubans, and the USA backing the anti-government group, UNITA. It wasn't until 1988, during numerous meetings convened by the USSR and USA, who were no longer engaged in the Cold War, that South Africa, Cuba and Angola edged towards an agreement. The Angolan government's fears of US support for the Unita rebel movement having been allayed, it was agreed that Cuban troops would begin a phased withdrawal from Angola; at the same time, South African soldiers would withdraw from Namibia.

The UN moved in to begin registering voters. The SWAPO leadership returned in June 1989, along with 40,000 exiles. In November that year elections were held for the National Assembly, which would write the new nation's constitution. In what are agreed to have been generally free and fair elections the SWAPO party of the Ovambos won decisively, but without the two-thirds majority it needed to write the constitution in their favour. This considerably calmed the fears of the German and Afrikaner communities, as well as those of the

Hereros and other minority tribes. On 21 March 1990, in the presence of Perez de Cuellar, the Secretary General of the UN, F. W. De Klerk, the South African President, and Sam Nujoma, ex-freedom fighter, now the country's first President, the Namibian flag was proudly run up the pole.

## THE PRESENT DAY

Namibia continues along democratic lines. It is a stable, peaceful country with a population of around 1.5 million, 10 per cent of whom are white. While the German-, Afrikaans- and English-speaking communities enjoy a disproportionate share of the wealth (80 per cent of gross national product), average per capita income for black Namibians is one of the highest in Africa. This is achieved with the not inconsiderable help of the diamond industry, which pays 12 per cent of all state tax revenue; it is in fact the biggest taxpayer, exporter (30 per cent of total) and – outside the government – employer. The enclave of Walvis Bay, which had come South Africa's way in 1910 when the Cape Colony joined the Union of South Africa, has now also joined the Republic of Namibia. Its incorporation has perhaps doubled the value of Namibia's manufacturing capacity. It is the base for an important fishing industry – the whales having been all but wiped out – and a major gateway for the country's other exports, which include uranium, copper, tin, beef, and the exquisitely soft pelts of Karakul lambs.

A word or two for those seeking enlightenment as to who owns what in the diamond industry: during the First World War Stauch, the railwayman whose discoveries started the diamond rush in 1908, had come to realize that the German diamond fields might be expropriated by the victorious Allies. The South West African mines should, he felt, be merged with South African interests. With his agreement Ernest Oppenheimer, acting on behalf of the Anglo-American Corporation of South Africa Ltd, acquired control of them in 1920, amalgamating the various mining interests into Consolidated Diamond Mines of South West Africa Ltd (CDM). Oppenheimer steered the industry through the market crash of the Thirties, creating the Central Selling Organization, the CSO, a powerful body which still controls 80 per cent of the world market in diamonds. In 1931 De Beers bought Anglo-American's interest in CDM, which became a subsidiary of De Beers in 1975. In November 1994, the government acquired a half share in CDM, and the company has been renamed Namdeb.

# SELECT
# BIBLIOGRAPHY

***The Chronology of Namibia,*** Hermann Kolberg (Society of Scientific Development, Windhoek, 1993). A convenient booklet marking key events – useful in a country rather bereft of up-to-date historical accounts.

***Diamonds in the Desert:*** *The Story of August Stauch and His Times,* Olga Levinson (Tafelberg Publishers, Cape Town, 1983). The best overview of the history of the diamond fields, from the Rush to the present. Well illustrated.

***Ecology of Desert Organisms,*** G.N. Louw and M.K. Seely (Longman, London, 1982). Slightly more specialist read by two leading authorities.

***Environmental Implications of Prospecting and Mining in the Namib,*** various authors (Geological Survey of Namibia Subdivision Publications, Windhoek, 1990). Academic discusson of a topic vital to the future of the Namib.

***Ephemeral Rivers and Their Catchments:*** *Sustaining People and Development in Western Namibia,* Peter J. Jacobson, Kathryn M. Jacobson and Mary K. Seely (Desert Research Foundation of Namibia, Windhoek, 1995). Excellent, well-illustrated book – up-to-date, pithy, but accessible.

***Himba:*** *Nomads in Namibia,* M. Jacobsohn and P. Pickford (C. Struik, Cape Town, 1990).

The definitive account of the Himba for general readers.

***Kamele in Südwestafrika,*** Ursula Massman (Namib und Meer, 1981, Vol. 9, pp. 31–54, Swakopmund; in German). Valuable, but only for camel devotees.

***Kolmanskop to Elizabeth Bay:*** *a Namdeb Guide,* G. Williamson (Namdeb Diamond Corporation Ltd, Oranjemund, 1995). Also ***Kolmanskop to Bogenfels:*** *a CDM Guide,* G. Williamson (CDM Ltd, Oranjemund, 1994). These two accessible pamphlets are published by CDM Namdeb, which also produces various slim publications such as a quarterly magazine called ***Ewi: The Voice of Namdeb***, a first-class source of up-to-date information on the diamond industry, and also interesting related aspects by authorities such as the archaeologist Dr Dieter Noli.

***Namib:*** *Dawn to Twilight,* Sylvie Bergerot, Eric Robert (Southern Book Publishers, Johannesburg, 1989). Glossy book with text à la *National Geographic*, but useful notes on Himba social structure and belief.

***Namib,*** David Coulson (Sidgwick and Jackson, London, 1991). By far the most thorough photographic record of the Namib; also perhaps the most comprehensive text.

***The Namib:*** *Natural History of an Ancient Desert,* Mary Seely (Shell Namibia Ltd, 1987).

The most handy guide for any tourist to the desert. Written by the foremost expert on the Namib, who has now published over seventy papers on the desert's ecology. DERU, the Desert Ecological Research Unit, where Seely is based, issue a bibliography (1952–1989), for academic researchers.

*Namibia: Africa's Harsh Paradise,* A. Bannister and P. Johnson (C. Struik Publishers, Cape Town, 1978). Good, well-illustrated, general read.

*Proceedings of Namibia's National Workshop to Combat Desertification,* ed. Stephanie Wolters (Desert Research Foundation of Namibia, Windhoek, 1994). Enlightened discussion of this important subject.

*The Sheltering Desert,* Henno Martin (AD. Donker Ltd, Craighall, 1983). A good read – account of two Germans sheltering from internment by the Allies in the Namib's Kuiseb River.

*Skeleton Coast,* Amy Schoeman (Southern Book Publishers, Johannesburg, 1984). Informed, well illustrated. The best overview on the 'Namibian Namib' by a local.

*Southern and Central Namibia in Jonker Afrikaner's Time,* Brigitte Lau (Windhoek Archives Publication Series No. 8, John Meinert Ltd, Windhoek, 1987). Account of a time (1800–1870) ignored by many historians and giving a concise insight into pre-colonial life.

The following publications were referred to in the text:

*Challenging the Namib Dune Sea*, Dr D.H.R. Hellwig (Namibia Scientific Society Newsletter, Vol. 31, No. 910, Sept.–Oct. 1990).

*Diamond Beaches: a History of Oranjemund 1928–1989*, Alison Corbett (A. Corbett, Claremont, 1989). A rare but extraordinarily detailed record.

*The Kalahari and its Lost City,* A.J. Clement (Longmans, Cape Town. 1967).

*Kalahari, Life's Variety in Dune and Delta,* Michael Main (Southern Book Publishers, Johannesburg, 1987).

*A Recent Journey in the Kalahari,* G.A. Farini (Proceedings of the Royal Geographical Society, 2nd Series, Vol. 18, 1886).

*Eine Reise längs der Küste Lüderitzbucht–Swakopmund im Februar–März 1912,* Dr E. Reuning (Mitteilungen aus den deutschen Schutzgebieten 26, 118–126, 1913; in German).

*Through the Kalahari Desert,* G.A. Farini (Sampson, Low, Marston, Searle and Rivington, London, 1886).

# ACKNOWLEDGEMENTS

First and foremost, I would like to thank the people of Namibia for being so generous in their attitude towards a foreigner, fortunate enough to be given the chance to undertake such a journey. The encouragement given me by Woker Freight Services, Air Namibia, and Skeleton Coast Safaris was astounding – yet typical of the country.

Second, I owe a lifelong debt to photographer Adrian Arbib, who in the end clung on for me in Namibia, keeping me going with moral and practical aid, for the entire expedition. From his first contacts, Bertus Schoeman in the UK and John van Bergen in Namibia, there emerged a spreading network of support. Bob Long, from VideoDiaries, championed the idea, while on the research side, Angela Fisher and David Coulson selflessly gave very useful early thoughts. Bärbel Kirchner of Namibia Tourism adopted the project and steered through the eventual ministerial permission via the Permanent Secretary, Hanno Rumpf, who gave me the government's endorsement and trust. Abel Gower, for Namdeb, did the same in the sensitive and highly restricted Sperrgebiet. From the moment permission was granted, André Pierre Marais, also from Namdeb in Windhoek, became a central bastion and friend.

As the reconnaissance trips got under way the kind Poolman family adopted me, and both John and Maria time and again propped me up. Above all, the Schoemans took me under their wing – I hope André's vital role with Bertus becomes clear in this book, and I would also like to thank Richard Engberts and Henk and Leon for their warm encouragement and help. Bärbel Schwarze coordinated all their support, and Jeanita Schoeman became a close friend of both me and the camels. Geraldine Delaney tirelessly liaised at Namdeb, while Janet Lewis organized me in Walvis Bay. Harald Dennewill, managing director of Woker Freight Services, stepped in to help with supply depots, passing me into the hands of the incomparable Günter Kock, director of International Stevedoring, who provided vital ground support and also transport to the Himbas.

Christo Bredenkamp steered me through my time in Oranjemund, with the help of Mike Lain, Rozane Demmer, and Elise Bredenkamp. Mike Wittet, the general manager, also took a personal interest, for example allowing the company horse trailer to make a rough excursion into the Kalahari to pick up the camels. Jan Coetzer established a wonderful temporary camel refuge for their arrival at the Orange River and the start of the journey. Gary Cowan provided a beautiful camel home among his beloved horses at our next port of call, Lüderitz, and also revitalized Adrian and myself. In Walvis Bay it was Heinke Kleyenstüber and the kind ladies of the stables who took them in, showing the mischievous camels hospitality that was, frankly, more than they deserved. John and Maria sprung into action and nurtured us yet again, along with Wayne, Stephanie, Karen and Melissa. Kraai Krause and Patrick Eagleton stoked up the camels and me, launching us out with aplomb into the desert again.

I would also like to thank, very sincerely, members of the conservation world who gave me their thoughts and time: the Minister of Environment and Tourism, Gert Hanekom, and the new Permanent Secretary, Ulitalah Hiveluah; Danie Grobler, who went out of his way to help, as did Rodney Braby, John Patterson, Chris Eyre, Rudi Loutit and Garth Owen-Smith; Palmwag Lodge, who allowed me through their exquisite concession area, also Johnny Roberts and David Stirling from Save the Rhino International, and Blythe Loutit and many staff from the Save the Rhino Trust. I should like, in particular, to mention the heroic Mike Hearn, who, in addition to helping me out with logistics, has, in company with Vanessa Buxton, just finished walking the camels safely out of the Kunene region. They are now in a luxurious kraal built by Save the Rhino, who will use the camels for anti-poaching patrols until Jeanita takes them on. My gratitude to Tommy Hall is, I hope, clear from the text. He gave me unstinting support and all the benefit of his expertise, despite my moans and groans. It emerged that he was a very special man, someone whom Marion and their children must be proud of. I also owe a debt to the man of the dunes, Joachim ('Achim') Lenssen, who was extraordinarily generous to me with his time and knowledge. I am sorry that, in the heat of the journey, my gratitude to him wasn't expressed as fully as I would have liked. He was right to be sceptical about whether the camels and I would last the trip.

I would particularly like to express my gratitude to the K. Blundell Trust, which awarded me a bursary to write this book, also the Royal Anthropological Institute, Virginia Luling of Survival International and also Effa Okupa and David Crandall for notes on the Himba. During the planning stage, Air Namibia was flying me back and forward to England, while Keith Woosey in the UK and Eddie Moutong, Usi and Thys went to enormous lengths to get the expedition up and running. Jason Goodwin and Kate Harris gave me a home base in London when I was broke and Tony Fox and Chloë Cunningham, as always, lent their organizational experience and support. I would like to say a special thanks also to John Whiston and David Taylor for trusting me somehow to present and write, between the recces, a railway-journey programme in E. Africa; George Chignell and Nicky Colton for helping me get through that nightmare schedule; Jo Sexton who helped sustain me while writing this book; Giles Oakley at the BBC's Community Programme Unit, which treated me as family – in particular Bob Long, Patrice Fentiman, my producer, Salim Salam, the technical men, Andy Collins and Jon Attard, and Tammi Cudmore-Ray. I would also like to thank the patient editors of this book, Martha Caute and Anna Ottewill, the book designer, Graham Dudley, David Cottingham for his skill in selecting photos and Bill Games for his expertise in checking the identification of the species encountered on my journey. Many institutions and individuals in Namibia, South Africa and the UK helped with identification, including Gillian Maggs, Director of the National Botanical Research Institute, Windhoek, Dr Robert Prys-Jones and Mark Adams (Walter Rothschild Zoological Museum, Tring); Dr Graham Williamson assisted with Sperrgebiet species, and Dr Paul Cornelius (Natural History Museum, London) with jellyfish. Elke Erb's gentle touch with camels gave me the confidence to train my own team myself, and without being unkind; when I arrived to undertake the training, Willie Knoesen and Esbé made a warm home for me in the Kalahari. Dieter Noli went out of his way to back us up, while Gino Noli also very kindly allowed me to wander with my camels over the Kolmanskop ghost town. Mary Seely of the Desert Ecological Research Unit was also very generous with her time. My treasured IBM laptop 'Thinkpad' has now safely seen me through the organizational phases of expeditions to the Amazon, Kenya, Uganda and Namibia, and I would like to thank IBM for seeing me through these jungles, savannahs and sands.

I would also like to extend a word of thanks to Akiko Ono; she, like the book *Beyond Siberia*, by writer and traveller Christina Dodwell, gave me inspiration at the beginning of my journey, after my mother had died on Christmas Day and when I had lost some of my spark to carry on. After the expedition, nearing this anniversary, Keith Woosey and Air Namibia again stepped in to help, flying my father out to Namibia to join me. Then, Bertus and André Schoeman generously invited both of us on one their unforgettable Skeleton Coast safaris. It is a supreme experience for any tourist to fly over this desert under their expert guidance; we were rewarded by the sight not only of elephants and ethereal dunes, but also of the recent tracks of three wandering camels and one exasperated human.

# FAUNA
# AND FLORA

ANIMALS AND PLANTS IDENTIFIED FROM THE AUTHOR'S JOURNEY.
*Page numbers in italic refer to illustration captions.*

**ANIMALS**

antelope (64, 138) family Bovidae

baboon (147, 155) (in general *Papio* spp. – also specifics listed separately)

baboon spider (159) family Theraphosidae

barking gecko (92) *Ptenopus garrulus*

bat-eared fox (53, 92) *Otocyon megalotis*

bee (168, 204) probably honeybee *Apis mellifera*

black-backed jackal (68, 72, *75*, 76, 78, 92, 109, 158, 196) *Canis mesomelas*

black mussel (101) *Choromytilus meridionalis*

brown hyena/strandwolf (72, *75*, 77, 78, 92, 101, 103, 109, 153) *Hyaena brunnea*

Burchell's/plains zebra (146) *Equus burchelli*

Cape fox (53, 92) *Vulpes chama*

Cape fur seal (*71*, 77, 102, 105, 109, 197) *Arctocephalus pusillus*

Cape hare (92, 139, 143, 187) *Lepus capensis*

chacma baboon (162, 163) *Papio ursinus*

crayfish (101) *Jasus lalandii*

cricket (151) *Acanthoplus* spp. and *Hetrodes* spp.

crocodile (186–7, 196–7, *199*, *207,* 208) *Crocodylus niloticus*

dolphin (*71*, 112) family Delphinidae

donkey (64) (African wild ass) *Equus asinus*

dung beetle (69) family Scarabaeidae

eland (53) *Taurotragus oryx*

elephant (African) (117, 153, 155, *157*, 162, 163–7, *169*) *Loxodonta africana*

elephant shrew (96) *Macroscelides proboscideus*

fog-basking beetle (100) *Onymacris unguicularis*

frog (208) *Tomopterna cryptotis*

gazelle (40, 68) (in general *Gazella* spp.)

gemsbok/oryx (61, 64, 88, 138, 143, 151, 152, *152, 153*, 158, 163) *Oryx gazella*

gerbil (92, 201, 203) (in general *Gerbillus* spp. – also specifics listed separately)

ghost crab (195) *Ocypode africana* and *O. cursor*

giraffe (*152, 157*, 162, 163, 164, 167) *Giraffa camelopardalis*

golden mole (92, 93) *Eremitalpa granti*

green turtle (197) *Chelonia mydas*

hairy-footed gerbil (190) *Gerbillurus paeba*

Hartmann's mountain zebra (146) *Equus zebra hartmannae*

horned adder (68, 128) *Bitis caudalis*

humpback whale (100) *Megaptera novaeangliae*

jellyfish (112–13) almost certainly *Desmonema* spp., but otherwise *Cyanea capillata*

kudu (143, 162) *Tragelaphus strepsiceros*

legless lizard (92) *Typhlacontias* spp.

lion (13, 117, 125, 139, 141, 150–1, 152, 154, 155, 159, *164*) *Panthera leo*

locust (40) family Acrididae

Namaqua chameleon (131, *136*) *Chamaeleo namaquensis*

Namib sand snake (144) *Psammophis leightoni namibensis*

*Onymacris plana* (100) a particular tenebrionid beetle

palmato gecko (93) *Palmatogecko rangei*

porcupine (90, 92, 146) *Hystrix africaeaustralis*

*Probergrothius sexpunctatis* (134) a bug with no common name

puff adder (144) *Bitis arietans*

red padloper tortoise (69) *Homopus bergeri*

reduviid/assassin bug (134) family Reduviidae

rhinoceros (116–17, 141–3, 151, 154, 155, 159, 162) *Diceros bicornis*

rockrabbit/hyrax/dassie (52, *54*) *Procavia capensis*

sand snake (89) (in general *Psammophis* spp. – also specifics listed separately)

shovel-nosed lizard/Namib sand-diver (100, 191) *Aporosaura anchietae*

sidewinder adder (92, 93) *Bitis peringueyi*

spotted hyena (153) *Crocuta crocuta*

springbok (68, 138, 143, 151, 157, 162) *Antidorcas marsupialis*

steenbok (68) *Raphicerus campestris*

tenebrionid beetle (93) (in general *Onymacris* spp. – also specifics listed separately)

western barred spitting cobra/zebra snake

# INDEX